MAP

Also by Wisława Szymborska

Here

Monologue of a Dog

Nonrequired Reading: Prose Pieces

Poems New and Collected, 1957–1997

View with a Grain of Sand: Selected Poems

Wisława Szymborska

MAP

Collected and Last Poems

Translated from the Polish by

Clare Cavanagh and Stanisław Barańczak

Edited by Clare Cavanagh

Mariner Books
Houghton Mifflin Harcourt
Boston New York

FUNDACJA WISŁAWY SZYMBORSKIEJ www.szymborska.org.pl

First Mariner Books edition 2016

www.hmhco.com

Library of Congress Cataloging-in-Publication Data
Names: Szymborska, Wisława, author.
Title: Map : collected and last poems / Wisława Szymborska ;
translated from the Polish by Clare Cavanagh and Stanisław Barańczak ;
edited by Clare Cavanagh.
Description: Boston : Houghton Mifflin Harcourt, 2015.
Identifiers: LCCN 2015297265 (print) | ISBN 978-0-544-12602-2 (hardcover) |
ISBN 978-0-544-70515-9 (trade paper) | ISBN 978-0-544-12777-7 (ebook)
Subjects: LCSH: Polish poetry—20th century. | Polish poetry—21st century.
Classification: LCC PG7178.Z9 A2 2015 (print) | LCC PG7178.Z9 (ebook) |
DDC 891.8/5173
LC record available at http://lccn.loc.gov/2015297265

Printed in the United States of America
DOC 10 9 8 7 6 5 4 3 2 1

All translations in this edition were made by Clare Cavanagh or Clare Cavanagh and Stanisław Barańczak

Contents

FROM UNPUBLISHED COLLECTION 1944-1948

* * *

Once we had the world backwards and forwards:
— it was so small it fit in two clasped hands,
so simple that a smile did to describe it,
so common, like old truths echoing in prayers.

History didn't greet us with triumphal fanfares:
— it flung dirty sand into our eyes.
Ahead of us lay long roads leading nowhere,
poisoned wells and bitter bread.

Our wartime loot is knowledge of the world,
— it is so large it fits in two clasped hands,
so hard that a smile does to describe it,
so strange, like old truths echoing in prayers.

Leaving the Movie Theater

Dreams flickered on white canvas.
The moon's husk glimmered for two hours.
There was the melancholy song of love,
a happy journey's end and flowers.

After the fairy tale, the world is hazy, blue.
The roles and faces here are unrehearsed.
The soldier sings the partisan's laments.
The young girl plays her songs of mourning too.

I'm coming back to you, the real world,
crowded, dark, and full of fate —
you, one-armed boy beneath the gate,
you, empty eyes of a young girl.

Comic Love Poem

I wear beads around my neck.
Every day's a day of joy
sustained by the touch
of unforeseen events.

I only know the rhythm
to a melody so soft
that if you ever heard it,
you'd have to hum along.

I exist not in myself,
I'm an element's function.
A symbol in the air.
Or a circle on the water.

Each time your eyes open,
I only take what's mine.
I leave faithfully behind
your earth, your fire.

Black Song

The long-drawn saxophonist, the saxophonist joker,
he's got his system for the world, he does fine without words.
The future — who can guess it. The past — who's got it right.
Just blink those thoughts away and play a black song.

They were dancing cheek to cheek. When someone dropped.
Head struck floor to the beat. They danced by him in time.
He didn't see the knees above him. Pale eyelids dawned,
plucked from the packed crowd, the night's strange colors.

Don't make a scene. He'll live. He must have drunk too much,
the blood by his temple must be lipstick. Nothing happened.
Just some guy on the floor. He fell himself, he'll get himself up,
he made it through the war. They danced on in cramped
    sweetness,
revolving fans mixed cold and heat,
the saxophone howled like a dog to a pink lantern.

FROM

WHY WE LIVE

1952

In Trite Rhymes

A great joy: flower upon flower,
the branches stretch in pristine blue,
but there's a greater: today's Tuesday,
tomorrow will bring mail from you,
and still greater: the letter trembles,
strange reading it in spots of sun,
and still greater: just a week now,
now just four days, now it's begun,
and still greater: I kneel on top
and make the suitcase lid shut tight,
and still greater: the train at seven,
just one ticket, thanks, that's right,
and still greater: rushing windows,
with view on view on view on view,
and still greater: dark and darker,
by nighttime I will be with you,
and still greater: the door opens,
and still greater: past the door,
and still greater: flower on flower.
—Ohhh, who are all these roses for?

Circus Animals

The marching bears hit all their notes,
the lion jumps through flaming hoops,
chimps ride their bikes in yellow coats,
the whip cracks and the trumpet toots.
The whip cracks, animal eyes leap,
an elephant strides, pitcher on his head,
dogs minuet with cautious feet.

We humans should be better bred.

So this was the great circus trip:
applause cascaded, just as planned,
an arm made longer by a whip
cast its sharp shadow on the sand.

FROM

QUESTIONS YOU ASK YOURSELF

1954

Questions You Ask Yourself

What do a smile and
handshake hold?
Do your greetings never
keep you as far
apart as other people
sometimes are
when passing judgment
at first glance?
Do you open each human
fate like a book,
seeking feelings
not in fonts
or formats?
Are you sure you
decipher people completely?
You gave an evasive
word in answering,
a bright joke in place of openness —
how do you tally your losses?
Stunted friendships,
frozen worlds.
Do you know that friendship,
like love, requires teamwork?
Someone missed a step
in this demanding effort.
In your friends' errors
do you bear no blame?
Someone complained, advised.

How many tears ran dry
before you lent a hand?
Jointly responsible
for the happiness of millennia,
don't you slight
the single minute
of a tear, a wince?
Do you never overlook
another's effort?
A glass stood on the table,
no one noticed
until it fell,
toppled by a thoughtless gesture.

Are people really so simple
as far as people go?

Lovers

In this quiet we can still hear
what they were singing yesterday
about the high road and the low road . . .
We hear — but we don't believe it.

Our smile doesn't mask our sorrow,
and goodness needs no sacrifice.
The pity we give to nonlovers
is even more than they deserve.

We're so astonished at ourselves,
what's left to astonish us?
Not a rainbow in the night.
Not a butterfly in snow.

And when we sleep
we dream of parting.
But it's a good dream,
it's a good dream,
since we wake up from it.

Key

The key was here and now it's gone.
How on earth do we get in?
Someone else may spot the key,
think, what's it got to do with me,
then pick it up and walk along
tossing the little scrap of tin.

If the same thing ever happened
to the love I have for you,
who'd be the poorer by this one love?
The whole world, not just we two.
Nothing but a simple form
picked up by another hand,
it won't open any door,
so let the rust do what it can.

No cards or stars or peacock's cries:
this horoscope can't end otherwise.

CALLING OUT TO YETI

1957

Night

And he said, Take now thy son, thine only son Isaac, whom thou lovest, and get thee into the land of Moriah; and offer him there for a burnt offering upon one of the mountains which I will tell thee of.

So what did Isaac do?
I ask the priest at catechism.
Break the neighbor's window with his ball?
Tear his new pants
on the fence post?
Did he steal pencils?
Scare the chickens?
Cheat on tests?

Leave the grownups
to their stupid sleep,
I've got to keep
watch until dawn.
The night is mute
but mute out of malice
and black
as the zeal of Abraham.

Where will I hide,
when God's biblical eye
lands on me
as it landed on Isaac?
Ancient history.
God can resurrect you if he wants.
I pull the blanket over my head
in a chill of fear.

Something white
will flit along the window,
then rustle through the room,

like a bird or the wind.
But no bird has
such enormous wings,
no wind wears
such a long gown.

The Lord God will pretend
he flew in by accident,
there must be some mistake,
then he'll take my father
to the kitchen and hatch plots,
blow a giant trumpet in his ear.

And at the crack of dawn
my father will drag me along,
I'll go, I'll go,
dark with hatred.

More defenseless
than November leaves,
I won't believe in goodness
or love.
No trust,
nothing can be trusted.
No caring,
no more live heart in my chest.
When it happens, as it has to happen,
when it happens,
a dried mushroom will be beating,
not a heart.

The Lord God waits,
from a balcony of clouds he checks,
does the stake light,
is it nice and even,
and he sees
how to die out of spite,
since I'll die,
refusing to be saved!

From that night
much worse than any bad dream,
from that night
much worse than loneliness,
the Lord God began
inch by inch
day by day
to move
from literalness
to metaphor.

Hania

Now see, here's Hania, the good servant.
And those aren't frying pans, you know, they're halos.
And that's a holy image, knight and serpent.
The serpent means vanity in this vale of woes.

And that's no necklace, that's her rosary.
Her shoes have toes turned up from daily kneeling.
Scarf dark as all the nights she sits up, weary,
and waits to hear the morning church bells pealing.

Scrubbing the mirror once, she saw a devil:
Bless me, Father, he shot a nasty look.
Blue with yellow stripes, eyes black as kettles —
you don't think he'll write me in his book?

And so she gives at Mass, she prays the mysteries,
and buys a small heart with a silver flame.
Since work began on the new rectory,
the devils have all run away in shame.

The cost is high, preserving souls from sin,
but only old folks come here, scraping by.
With so much of nothing, razor-thin,
Hania would vanish in the Needle's Eye.

May, renounce your hues for wintery gray.
Leafy bough, throw off your greenery.
Clouds, repent; sun, cast your beams away.
Spring, save your blooms for heaven's scenery.

I never heard her laughter or her tears.
Raised humble, she owns nothing but her skin.
A shadow walks beside her — her mortal fears,
her tattered kerchief yammers in the wind.

Nothing Twice

Nothing can ever happen twice.
In consequence, the sorry fact is
that we arrive here improvised
and leave without the chance to practice.

Even if there is no one dumber,
if you're the planet's biggest dunce,
you can't repeat the class in summer:
this course is only offered once.

No day copies yesterday,
no two nights will teach what bliss is
in precisely the same way,
with exactly the same kisses.

One day, perhaps, some idle tongue
mentions your name by accident:
I feel as if a rose were flung
into the room, all hue and scent.

The next day, though you're here with me,
I can't help looking at the clock:
A rose? A rose? What could that be?
Is it a flower or a rock?

Why do we treat the fleeting day
with so much needless fear and sorrow?
It's in its nature not to stay:
today is always gone tomorrow.

With smiles and kisses, we prefer
to seek accord beneath our star,
although we're different (we concur)
just as two drops of water are.

Flagrance

So here we are, the naked lovers,
lovely, as we both agree,
with eyelids as our only covers
we lie in the dark, invisibly.

But they already know, they know,
all four corners, the night air,
the upright table and the stove,
suspicious shadows fill the chairs.

The tea grows cold; the cups know why,
although the reason's left unsaid.
Swift must lay his hopes aside,
his book lies open, but unread.

As for the birds? I saw them flying
yesterday as, without shame,
they scrawled across the open sky
the letters spelling out your name.

As for the trees? Well, can't you hear
what they keep whispering about?
You say it's in the atmosphere,
but how'd the atmosphere find out?

A moth flies in the open window
on furry wings, it hovers first,
then soars above and swoops below,
and stubbornly hums over us.

Perhaps it catches what we miss
with its uncanny insect sight?
I didn't see, you didn't guess,
our hearts were glowing in the night.

Buffo

First, our love will die, alas,
then two hundred years will pass,
then we'll meet again at last—

this time in the theater, played
by a couple of comedians,
him and her, the public's darlings.

Just a little farce, with songs,
patter, jokes, and final bows,
a vaudeville comedy of manners,
certain to bring down the house.

You'll amuse them endlessly
on the stage with your cravat
and your petty jealousy.

So will I, love's silly pawn,
with my heart, my joy, my crown,
my heart broken, my joy gone,
my crown tumbling to the ground.

To the laughter's loud refrain,
we will meet and part again,
seven mountains, seven rivers
multiplying our pain.

If we haven't had enough
of despair, grief, all that stuff,
lofty words will kill us off.

Then we'll stand up, take our bows:
hope that you've enjoyed our show.
Every patron with his spouse
will applaud, get up, and go.

They'll reenter their lives' cages,
where love's tiger sometimes rages,
but the beast's too tame to bite.

We'll remain the odd ones out,
silly heathens in their fools' caps,
listening to the small bells ringing
day and night.

Commemoration

They made love in a hazel grove,
beneath the little suns of dew;
dry leaves and twigs got in their hair
and dry dirt too.

Swallow's heart, have
mercy on them.

They both knelt down on the lakeshore,
they combed the dry leaves from their hair;
small fish, a star's converging rays,
swam up to stare.

Swallow's heart, have
mercy on them.

Reflected in the rippling lake,
trees trembled, nebulous and gray;
O swallow, let them never, never
forget this day.

O swallow, cloud-borne thorn,
anchor of the air,
Icarus improved,
coattails in Assumption,

O swallow, calligraphy,
clockhand minus minutes,
early ornithogothic,
heaven's cross-eyed glance,

O swallow, knife-edged silence,
mournful exuberance,
the aureole of lovers,
have mercy on them.

Classifieds

WHOEVER'S found out what location
compassion (heart's imagination)
can be contacted at these days
is herewith urged to name the place,
and sing about it in full voice,
and dance like crazy and rejoice
beneath the frail birch that appears
to be upon the verge of tears.

I TEACH silence
in all languages
through intensive examination of:
the starry sky,
the Sinanthropus's jaws,
a grasshopper's hop,
an infant's fingernails,
plankton,
a snowflake.

I RESTORE lost love.
Act now! Special offer!
You lie on last year's grass
bathed in sunlight to the chin
while winds of summers past
caress your hair and seem
to lead you in a dance.
For further details, write: "Dream."

WANTED: someone to mourn
the elderly who die
alone in old folks' homes.
Applicants, don't send forms
or birth certificates.
All papers will be torn,
no receipts will be issued
at this or later dates.

FOR PROMISES made by my spouse,
who's tricked so many with his sweet
colors and fragrances and sounds—
dogs barking, guitars in the street—
into believing that they still
might conquer loneliness and fright,
I cannot be responsible.
Mr. Day's widow, Mrs. Night.

Moment of Silence

Wait, you can't go in there,
it's all smoke and flames!
— Four kids got trapped inside,
I'm going in for them!

So how do you
suddenly lose the habit
of yourself?
of day follows night?
of the snows of yesteryear?
of rosy apples?
of the yearning for love,
which is never enough?

No goodbyes on either side,
she goes to help the kids alone,
she wades through fire to her thighs,
she grabs them up and swings them high,
her hair catches the flames' glow.

But she'd wanted to buy a ticket,
take a quick vacation,
write a letter,
open the window after a storm,
beat a track through the woods,
admire ants,
watch the lake
blinking in the wind.

A moment of silence for the dead
can take all night.

I've borne witness
to the flight of clouds and birds,
I hear grass growing
and know what to call it,
I've read millions
of printed marks,
I've trained a telescope
along strange stars,
but no one so far
has called for my help,
and what if I regret
a leaf, a dress, a rhyme—

We know ourselves only
as far as we've been tested.
I tell you this
from my unknown heart.

Rehabilitation

I wield imagination's oldest right
and summon up the dead for the first time,
I watch for their faces, anticipate their steps,
though I know that dead is dead and gone.

It's time to take my head in hand
and say: Poor Yorick, where's your ignorance,
where's your blind faith, where's your innocence,
your wait-and-see, your spirit poised
between the unproved and the proven truth?

I believed in their betrayal, they didn't merit names,
since weeds sway on their unknown graves
and the crows mock them, and the snowflakes scoff
—but Yorick, all this bore false witness.

Tickets to the afterlife are paid
by our collective memory.
Uncertain coinage. Every day
some dead man's banished from eternity.

I see eternity more clearly now:
how we give it, how we strip it from
the so-called traitor—how
his name dies alongside of him.

We must give the dead due weight,
our power over them is what we make it:
this court cannot convene at night,
the judge presiding can't be naked.

The earth surges — those once turned to earth
rise up, clod by clod, a fistful at a time;
they leave silence behind, return to names,
to the nation's memory, to wreaths and cheers.

Where is my power over words?
Words fallen to a tear's depths,
words words not meant to conquer death,
dead record, like a photo with its magnesium flash.
I can't even restore them to half-breath,
a Sisyphus assigned to the hell of poetry.

They come to us. Sharp as diamonds,
they pass along shop windows lit in front,
along the windowpanes of cozy houses,
along rose-colored glasses, along the glass
of hearts and brains, quietly cutting.

To My Friends

Well versed in the expanses
that stretch from earth to stars,
we get lost in the space
from earth up to our skull.

Intergalactic reaches
divide sorrow from tears.
En route from false to true
you wither and grow dull.

We are amused by jets,
those crevices of silence
wedged between flight and sound:
"World record!" the world cheers.

But we've seen faster takeoffs:
their long-belated echo
still wrenches us from sleep
after so many years.

Outside, a storm of voices:
"We're innocent," they cry.
We rush to open windows,
lean out to catch their call.

But then the voices break off.
We watch the falling stars
just as after a salvo
plaster drops from the wall.

Funeral (I)

His skull, dug up from clay,
rests in a marble tomb;
sleep tight, medals, on pillows:
now it's got lots of room,
that skull dug up from clay.

They read off index cards:
a) he has been/will be missed,
b) go on, band, play the march,
c) too bad he can't see this.
They read off index cards.

Nation, be thankful now
for blessings you possess:
a being born just once
has two graves nonetheless.
Nation, be thankful now.

Parades were plentiful:
a thousand slide trombones,
police for crowd control,
bell-ringing for the bones.
Parades were plentiful.

Their eyes flicked heavenward
for omens from above:
a ray of light perhaps
or a bomb-carrying dove.
Their eyes flicked heavenward.

Between them and the people,
according to the plan,
the trees alone would sing
their silence on command.
Between them and the people.

Instead, bridges are drawn
above a gorge of stone,
its bed's been smoothed for tanks,
echoes await a moan.
Instead, bridges are drawn.

Still full of blood and hopes
the people turn away,
not knowing that bell ropes,
like human hair, turn gray.

Still full of blood and hopes.

* * *

I hear trumpets play the tune
to a history of woe.
For I lived once in the town
that is known as Jericho.

The walls, they all go tumbling,
tra ta ta, sounds the fanfare,
and I stand stripped to nothing
but a uniform of air.

So blow, you trumpets, blow true,
quickly, strike up the whole band.
My skin will fall away too,
only whitened bones will stand.

Brueghel's Two Monkeys

This is what I see in my dreams about final exams:
two monkeys, chained to the floor, sit on the windowsill,
the sky behind them flutters,
the sea is taking its bath.

The exam is History of Mankind.
I stammer and hedge.

One monkey stares and listens with mocking disdain,
the other seems to be dreaming away—
but when it's clear I don't know what to say
he prompts me with a gentle
clinking of his chain.

Still

Across the country's plains
sealed boxcars are carrying names:
how long will they travel, how far,
will they ever leave the boxcar —
don't ask, I can't say, I don't know.

The name Nathan beats the wall with his fist,
the name Isaac sings a mad hymn,
the name Aaron is dying of thirst,
the name Sarah begs water for him.

Don't jump from the boxcar, name David.
In these lands you're a name to avoid,
you're bound for defeat, you're a sign
pointing out those who must be destroyed.

At least give your son a Slavic name:
he'll need it. Here people count hairs
and examine the shape of your eyelids
to tell right from wrong, "ours" from "theirs."

Don't jump yet. Your son's name will be Lech.
Don't jump yet. The time's still not right.
Don't jump yet. The clattering wheels
are mocked by the echoes of night.

Clouds of people passed over this plain.
Vast clouds, but they held little rain —
just one tear, that's a fact, just one tear.
A dark forest. The tracks disappear.

That's-a-fact. The rail and the wheels.
That's-a-fact. A forest, no fields.
That's-a-fact. And their silence once more,
that's-a-fact, drums on my silent door.

Greeting the Supersonics

Faster than sound today,
faster than light tomorrow,
we'll turn sound into the Tortoise
and light into the Hare.

Two venerable creatures
from the ancient parable,
a noble team, since ages past
competing fair and square.

You ran so many times
across this lowly earth;
now try another course,
across the lofty blue.

The track's all yours. We won't
get in your way: by then
we will have set off chasing
ourselves rather than you.

Still Life with a Balloon

Returning memories?
No, at the time of death
I'd like to see lost objects
return instead.

Avalanches of gloves,
coats, suitcases, umbrellas —
come, and I'll say at last:
What good's all this?

Safety pins, two odd combs,
a paper rose, a knife,
some string — come, and I'll say
at last: I haven't missed you.

Please turn up, key, come out,
wherever you've been hiding,
in time for me to say:
You've gotten rusty, friend!

Downpours of affidavits,
permits and questionnaires,
rain down and I will say:
I see the sun behind you.

My watch, dropped in a river,
bob up and let me seize you —
then, face to face, I'll say:
Your so-called time is up.

And lastly, toy balloon
once kidnapped by the wind —
come home, and I will say:
There are no children here.

Fly out the open window
and into the wide world;
let someone else shout "Look!"
and I will cry.

Notes from a Nonexistent Himalayan Expedition

So these are the Himalayas.
Mountains racing to the moon.
The moment of their start recorded
on the startling, ripped canvas of the sky.
Holes punched in a desert of clouds.
Thrust into nothing.
Echo — a white mute.
Quiet.

Yeti, down there we've got Wednesday,
bread, and alphabets.
Two times two is four.
Roses are red there,
and violets are blue.

Yeti, crime is not all
we're up to down there.
Yeti, not every sentence there
means death.

We've inherited hope —
the gift of forgetting.
You'll see how we give
birth among the ruins.

Yeti, we've got Shakespeare there.
Yeti, we play solitaire
and violin. At nightfall,
we turn lights on, Yeti.

Up here it's neither moon nor earth.
Tears freeze.
Oh Yeti, semi-moonman,
turn back, think again!

I called this to the Yeti
inside four walls of avalanche,
stomping my feet for warmth
on the everlasting
snow.

An Effort

Alack and woe, oh song: you're mocking me;
try as I may, I'll never be your red, red rose.
A rose is a rose is a rose. And you know it.

I worked to sprout leaves. I tried to take root.
I held my breath to speed things up, and waited
for the petals to enclose me.

Merciless song, you leave me with my lone,
nonconvertible, unmetamorphic body:
I'm one-time-only to the marrow of my bones.

Four A.M.

The hour between night and day.
The hour between toss and turn.
The hour of thirty-year-olds.

The hour swept clean for roosters' crowing.
The hour when the earth takes back its warm embrace.
The hour of cool drafts from extinguished stars.
The hour of do-we-vanish-too-without-a-trace.

Empty hour.
Hollow. Vain.
Rock bottom of all the other hours.

No one feels fine at four A.M.
If ants feel fine at four A.M.,
we're happy for the ants. And let five A.M. come
if we've got to go on living.

Midsummer Night's Dream

The forest in the Vosges Mountains shines.
Don't come near me.
Foolish, foolish,
I've been consorting with the world.

I've eaten bread, I've drunk water,
the wind stroked me, the rain soaked me,
so beware and leave me.
And cover up your eyes.

Leave me, leave, but not by land.
Swim off, swim, but not by sea.
Fly off, fly away, my dear,
but don't go near the air.

Let's see each other through closed eyes.
Let's talk together through closed mouths.
Let's hold each other through a thick wall.

We don't make a pretty pair of clowns,
the forest, not the moon, is shining down,
and a gust tears from your lady thus
her radioactive coat, oh Pyramus.

Atlantis

They were or they weren't.
On an island or not.
An ocean or not an ocean
swallowed them up or it didn't.

Was there anyone to love anyone?
Did anybody have someone to fight?
Everything happened or it didn't
there or someplace else.

Seven cities stood there.
So we think.
They were meant to stand forever.
We suppose.

They weren't up to much, no.
They were up to something, yes.

Hypothetical. Dubious.
Uncommemorated.
Never extracted from air,
fire, water, or earth.

Not contained within a stone
or drop of rain.
Not suitable for straight-faced use
as a story's moral.

A meteor fell.
Not a meteor.
A volcano exploded.
Not a volcano.
Someone summoned something.
Nothing was called.

On this more-or-less Atlantis.

I'm Working on the World

I'm working on the world,
revised, improved edition,
featuring fun for fools,
blues for brooders,
combs for bald pates,
tricks for old dogs.

Here's one chapter: The Speech
of Animals and Plants.
Each species comes, of course,
with its own dictionary.
Even a simple "Hi there,"
when traded with a fish,
makes both the fish and you
feel quite extraordinary.

The long-suspected meanings
of rustlings, chirps, and growls!
Soliloquies of forests!
The epic hoots of owls!
Those crafty hedgehogs drafting
aphorisms after dark,
while we blindly believe
they're sleeping in the park!

Time (Chapter Two) retains
its sacred right to meddle
in each earthly affair.
Still, time's unbounded power
that makes a mountain crumble,
moves seas, rotates a star,

won't be enough to tear
lovers apart: they are
too naked, too embraced,
too much like timid sparrows.

Old age is, in my book,
the price that felons pay,
so don't whine that it's steep:
you'll stay young if you're good.
Suffering (Chapter Three)
doesn't insult the body.
Death? It comes in your sleep,
exactly as it should.

When it comes, you'll be dreaming
that you don't need to breathe;
that breathless silence is
the music of the dark
and it's part of the rhythm
to vanish like a spark.

Only a death like that. A rose
could prick you harder, I suppose;
you'd feel more terror at the sound
of petals falling to the ground.

Only a world like that. To die
just that much. And to live just so.
And all the rest is Bach's fugue, played
for the time being
on a saw.

SALT

1962

The Monkey

Evicted from the Garden long before
the humans: he had such infectious eyes
that just one glance around old Paradise
made even angels' hearts feel sad and sore,
emotions hitherto unknown to them.
Without a chance to say "I disagree,"
he had to launch his earthly pedigree.
Today, still nimble, he retains his charme
with a primeval "e" after the "m."

Worshiped in Egypt, pleiades of fleas
spangling his sacred and silvery mane,
he'd sit and listen in archsilent peace:
What do you want? A life that never ends?
He'd turn his ruddy rump as if to say
such life he neither bans nor recommends.

In Europe they deprived him of his soul
but they forgot to take his hands away;
there was a painter-monk who dared portray
a saint with palms so thin, they could be simian.
The holy woman prayed for heaven's favor
as if she waited for a nut to fall.

Warm as a newborn, with an old man's tremor,
imported to kings' courts across the seas,
he whined while swinging on his golden chain,
dressed in the garish coat of a marquis.
Prophet of doom. The court is laughing? Please.

Considered edible in China, he makes boiled
or roasted faces when laid upon a salver.
Ironic as a gem set in sham gold.
His brain is famous for its subtle flavor,
though it's no good for trickier endeavors,
for instance, thinking up gunpowder.

In fables, lonely, not sure what to do,
he fills up mirrors with his indiscreet
self-mockery (a lesson for us, too);
the poor relation, who knows all about us,
though we don't greet each other when we meet.

Lesson

Subject King Alexander *predicate* cuts *direct*
object the Gordian knot with his *indirect object* sword.
This had never *predicate* entered anyone's *object* mind before.

None of a hundred philosophers could disentangle this knot.
No wonder each now shrinks in some secluded spot.
The soldiers, loud and with great glee,
grab each one by his trembling gray goatee
and *predicate* drag *object* him out.

Enough's enough. The king calls for his horse,
adjusts his crested helm and sallies forth.
And in his wake, with trumpets, drums, and flutes,
his *subject* army made of little knots
predicate marches off to *indirect object* war.

Museum

Here are plates but no appetite.
And wedding rings, but the requited love
has been gone now for some three hundred years.

Here's a fan — where is the maiden's blush?
Here are swords — where is the ire?
Nor will the lute sound at the twilight hour.

Since eternity was out of stock,
ten thousand aging things have been amassed instead.
The moss-grown guard in golden slumber
props his mustache on the Exhibit Number . . .

Eight. Metals, clay, and feathers celebrate
their silent triumphs over dates.
Only some Egyptian flapper's silly hairpin giggles.

The crown has outlasted the head.
The hand has lost out to the glove.
The right shoe has defeated the foot.

As for me, I am still alive, you see.
The battle with my dress still rages on.
It struggles, foolish thing, so stubbornly!
Determined to keep living when I'm gone!

A Moment in Troy

Little girls —
skinny, resigned
to freckles that won't go away,

not turning any heads
as they walk across the eyelids of the world,

looking just like Mom or Dad,
and sincerely horrified by it —

in the middle of dinner,
in the middle of a book,
while studying the mirror,
may suddenly be taken off to Troy.

In the grand boudoir of a wink
they all turn into beautiful Helens.

They ascend the royal staircase
in the rustling of silk and admiration.
They feel light. They all know
that beauty equals rest,
that lips mold the speech's meaning,
and gestures sculpt themselves
in inspired nonchalance.

Their small faces
worth dismissing envoys for
extend proudly on necks
that merit countless sieges.

Those tall, dark movie stars,
their girlfriends' older brothers,
the teacher from art class,
alas, they must all be slain.

Little girls
observe disaster
from a tower of smiles.

Little girls
wring their hands
in intoxicating mock despair.

Little girls
against a backdrop of destruction,
with flaming towns for tiaras,
in earrings of pandemic lamentation.

Pale and tearless.
Triumphant. Sated with the view.
Dreading only the inevitable
moment of return.

Little girls
returning.

Shadow

My shadow is a fool whose feelings
are often hurt by his routine
of rising up behind his queen
to bump his silly head on ceilings.

His is a world of two dimensions,
that's true, but flat jokes still can smart;
he longs to flaunt my court's conventions
and drop a role he knows by heart.

The queen leans out above the sill,
the jester tumbles out for real:
thus they divide their actions; still,
it's not a fifty-fifty deal.

My jester took on nothing less
than royal gestures' shamelessness,
the things that I'm too weak to bear—
the cloak, crown, scepter, and the rest.

I'll stay serene, won't feel a thing,
yes, I will turn my head away
after I say goodbye, my king,
at railway station N., someday.

My king, it is the fool who'll lie
across the tracks; the fool, not I.

The Rest

Her mad songs over, Ophelia darts out,
anxious to check offstage whether her dress is
still not too crumpled, whether her blond tresses
frame her face as they should.

Since real life's laws
require facts, she, Polonius's true
daughter, carefully washes black despair
out of her eyebrows, and is not above
counting the leaves she's combed out of her hair.
Oh, may Denmark forgive you, my dear, and me too:
I'll die with wings, I'll live on with practical claws.
Non omnis moriar of love.

Clochard

In Paris, on a day that stayed morning until dusk,
in a Paris like —
in a Paris which —
(save me, sacred folly of description!)
in a garden by a stone cathedral
(not built, no, rather
played upon a lute)
a *clochard*, a lay monk, a naysayer,
sleeps sprawled like a knight in effigy.

If he ever owned anything, he has lost it,
and having lost it doesn't want it back.
He's still owed soldier's pay for the conquest of Gaul —
but he got over that, it doesn't matter.
And they never paid him in the fifteenth century
for posing as the thief on Christ's left hand —
he has forgotten all about it, he's not waiting.

He earns his red wine
by trimming the neighborhood dogs.
He sleeps with the air of an inventor of dreams,
his thick beard swarming toward the sun.

The gray chimeras (to wit, bulldogryphons,
hellephants, hippopotoads, croakodilloes, rhinocerberuses,
behemammoths, and demonopods,
that omnibestial Gothic *allegro vivace*)
unpetrify

and examine him with a curiosity
they never turn on me or you,
prudent Peter,
zealous Michael,
enterprising Eve,
Barbara, Clare.

Vocabulary

"*La Pologne? La Pologne?* Isn't it terribly cold there?" she asked, and then sighed with relief. So many countries have been turning up lately that the safest thing to talk about is climate.

"Madame," I want to reply, "my people's poets do all their writing in mittens. I don't mean to imply that they never remove them; they do, indeed, if the moon is warm enough. In stanzas composed of raucous whooping, for only such can drown the windstorms' constant roar, they glorify the simple lives of our walrus herders. Our Classicists engrave their odes with inky icicles on trampled snowdrifts. The rest, our Decadents, bewail their fate with snowflakes instead of tears. He who wishes to drown himself must have an ax at hand to cut the ice. Oh, madame, dearest madame."

That's what I mean to say. But I've forgotten the word for walrus in French. And I'm not sure of icicle and ax.

"*La Pologne? La Pologne?* Isn't it terribly cold there?"

"*Pas du tout,*" I answer icily.

Travel Elegy

Everything's mine but just on loan,
nothing for the memory to hold,
though mine as long as I look.

Memories come to mind like excavated statues
that have misplaced their heads.

From the town of Samokov, only rain
and more rain.

Paris from Louvre to fingernail
grows web-eyed by the moment.

Boulevard Saint-Martin: some stairs
leading into a fade-out.

Only a bridge and a half
from Leningrad of the bridges.

Poor Uppsala, reduced to a splinter
of its mighty cathedral.

Sofia's hapless dancer,
a form without a face.

Then separately, his face without eyes;
separately again, eyes with no pupils,
and, finally, the pupils of a cat.

A Caucasian eagle soars
above a reproduction of a canyon,
the fool's gold of the sun,
the phony stones.

Everything's mine but just on loan,
nothing for the memory to hold,
though mine as long as I look.

Inexhaustible, unembraceable,
but particular to the smallest fiber,
grain of sand, drop of water —
landscapes.

I won't retain one blade of grass
as it's truly seen.

Salutation and farewell
in a single glance.

For surplus and absence alike,
a single motion of the neck.

Without a Title

The two of them were left so long alone,
so much in un-love, without a word to spare,
what they deserve by now is probably
a miracle — a thunderbolt, or turning into stone.
Two million books in print on Greek mythology,
but there's no rescue in them for this pair.

If at least someone would ring the bell, or if
something would flare and disappear again,
no matter from where and no matter when,
no matter if it's fun, fear, joy, or grief.

But nothing of the sort. No aberration,
no deviation from the well-made plot
this bourgeois drama holds. There'll be a dot
above the "i" inside their tidy separation.

Against the backdrop of the steadfast wall,
pitying one another, they both stare
into the mirror, but there's nothing there
except their sensible reflections. All

they see is the two people in the frame.
Matter is on alert. All its dimensions,
everything in between the ground and sky
keeps close watch on the fates that we were born with
and sees to it that they remain the same —
although we still don't see the reason why
a sudden deer bounding across this room
would shatter the entire universe.

An Unexpected Meeting

We treat each other with exceeding courtesy;
we say, it's great to see you after all these years.

Our tigers drink milk.
Our hawks tread the ground.
Our sharks have all drowned.
Our wolves yawn beyond the open cage.

Our snakes have shed their lightning,
our apes their flights of fancy,
our peacocks have renounced their plumes.
The bats flew out of our hair long ago.

We fall silent in midsentence,
all smiles, past help.
Our humans
don't know how to talk to one another.

Golden Anniversary

They must have been different once,
fire and water, miles apart,
robbing and giving in desire,
that assault on one another's otherness.
Embracing, they appropriated and expropriated each other
for so long
that only air was left within their arms,
transparent as if after lightning.

One day the answer came before the question.
Another night they guessed their eyes' expression
by the type of silence in the dark.

Gender fades, mysteries molder,
distinctions meet in all-resemblance
just as all colors coincide in white.

Which of them is doubled and which missing?
Which one is smiling with two smiles?
Whose voice forms a two-part canon?
When both heads nod, which one agrees?
Whose gesture lifts the teaspoon to their lips?
Who's flayed the other one alive?
Which one lives and which has died
entangled in the lines of whose palm?

They gazed into each other's eyes and slowly twins emerged.
Familiarity breeds the most perfect of mothers —
it favors neither of the little darlings,
it scarcely can recall which one is which.

On this festive day, their golden anniversary,
a dove, seen identically, perched on the windowsill.

Starvation Camp Near Jaslo

Write it down. Write it. With ordinary ink
on ordinary paper: they weren't given food,
they all died of hunger. *All. How many?*
It's a large meadow. How much grass
per head? Write down: I don't know.
History rounds off skeletons to zero.
A thousand and one is still only a thousand.
That *one* seems never to have existed:
a fictitious fetus, an empty cradle,
a primer opened for no one,
air that laughs, cries, and grows,
stairs for a void bounding out to the garden,
no one's spot in the ranks.

It became flesh right here, on this meadow.
But the meadow's silent, like a witness who's been bought.
Sunny. Green. A forest close at hand,
with wood to chew on, drops beneath the bark to drink—
a view served round the clock,
until you go blind. Above, a bird
whose shadow flicked its nourishing wings
across their lips. Jaws dropped,
teeth clattered.

At night a sickle glistened in the sky
and reaped the dark for dreamed-of loaves.
Hands came flying from blackened icons,
each holding an empty chalice.

A man swayed
on a grill of barbed wire.
Some sang, with dirt in their mouths. *That lovely song*
about war hitting you straight in the heart.
Write how quiet it is.
Yes.

Parable

Some fishermen pulled a bottle from the deep. It held a piece of paper, with these words: "Somebody save me! I'm here. The ocean cast me on this desert island. I am standing on the shore waiting for help. Hurry! I'm here!"

"There's no date. I bet it's already too late anyway. It could have been floating for years," the first fisherman said.

"And he doesn't say where. It's not even clear which ocean," the second fisherman said.

"It's not too late, or too far. The island Here is everywhere," the third fisherman said.

They all felt awkward. No one spoke. That's how it goes with universal truths.

Ballad

Hear the ballad "Murdered Woman
Suddenly Gets Up from Chair."

It's an honest ballad, penned
neither to shock nor to offend.

The thing happened fair and square,
with curtains open, lamps all lit:

passersby could stop and stare.

When the door had shut behind him
and the killer ran downstairs,
she stood up, just like the living
startled by the sudden silence.

She gets up, she moves her head,
and she looks around with eyes
harder than they were before.

No, she doesn't float through air:
she steps on the ordinary,
wooden, slightly creaky floor.

In the oven she burns traces
that the killer's left behind:
here a picture, there shoelaces,
everything that she can find.

It's obvious that she's not strangled.
It's obvious that she's not shot.
She's been killed invisibly.

She may still show signs of life,
cry for sundry silly reasons,
shriek in horror at the sight
of a mouse.
                    Ridiculous
traits are so predictable
that they aren't hard to fake.

She got up like you and me.

She walks just as people do.

And she sings and combs her hair,
which still grows.

Over Wine

He glanced, gave me extra charm
and I took it as my own.
Happily I gulped a star.

I let myself be invented,
modeled on my own reflection
in his eyes. I dance, dance, dance
in the stir of sudden wings.

The chair's a chair, the wine is wine,
in a wineglass that's the wineglass
standing there by standing there.
Only I'm imaginary,
make-believe beyond belief,
so fictitious that it hurts.

And I tell him tales about
ants that die of love beneath
a dandelion's constellation.
I swear a white rose will sing
if you sprinkle it with wine.

I laugh and I tilt my head
cautiously, as if to check
whether the invention works.
I dance, dance inside my stunned
skin, in his arms that create me.

Eve from the rib, Venus from foam,
Minerva from Jupiter's head —
all three were more real than me.

When he isn't looking at me,
I try to catch my reflection
on the wall. And see the nail
where a picture used to be.

Rubens' Women

Titanettes, female fauna,
naked as the rumbling of barrels.
They roost in trampled beds,
asleep, with mouths agape, ready to crow.
Their pupils have fled into flesh
and sound the glandular depths
from which yeast seeps into their blood.

Daughters of the Baroque. Dough
thickens in troughs, baths steam, wines blush,
cloudy piglets careen across the sky,
triumphant trumpets neigh the carnal alarm.

O pumpkin plump! O pumped-up corpulence
inflated double by disrobing
and tripled by your tumultuous poses!
O fatty dishes of love!

Their skinny sisters woke up earlier,
before dawn broke and shone upon the painting.
And no one saw how they went single file
along the canvas's unpainted side.

Exiled by style. Only their ribs stood out.
With birdlike feet and palms, they strove
to take wing on their jutting shoulder blades.

The thirteenth century would have given them golden halos.
The twentieth, silver screens.
The seventeenth, alas, holds nothing for the unvoluptuous.

For even the sky bulges here
with pudgy angels and a chubby god—
thick-whiskered Phoebus, on a sweaty steed,
riding straight into the seething bedchamber.

Coloratura

Poised beneath a twig-wigged tree,
she spills her sparkling vocal powder:
slippery sound slivers, silvery
like spider's spittle, only louder.

Oh yes, she Cares (with a high C)
for Fellow Humans (you and me);
for us she'll twitter nothing bitter;
she'll knit her fitter, sweeter glitter;
her vocal cords mince words for us
and crumble croutons, with crisp crunch
(lunch for her little lambs to munch)
into a cream-filled demitasse.

But hark! It's dark! Oh doom too soon!
She's threatened by the black bassoon!
It's hoarse and coarse, it's grim and gruff,
it calls her dainty voice's bluff—
Basso Profundo, end this terror,
do-re-mi mene tekel et cetera!

You want to silence her, abduct her
to our chilly life behind the scenes?
To our Siberian steppes of stopped-up sinuses,
frogs in all throats, eternal hems and haws,
where we, poor souls, gape soundlessly
like fish? And this is what you wish?

Oh nay! Oh nay! Though doom be nigh,
she'll keep her chin and pitch up high!
Her fate is hanging by a hair
of voice so thin it sounds like *air*,
but that's enough for her to take
a breath and soar, without a break,
chandelierward; and while she's there,
her vox humana crystal-clears
the whole world up. And we're all ears.

Bodybuilders' Contest

From scalp to sole, all muscles in slow motion.
The ocean of his torso drips with lotion.
The king of all is he who preens and wrestles
with sinews twisted into monstrous pretzels.

Onstage, he grapples with a grizzly bear
the deadlier for not really being there.
Three unseen panthers are in turn laid low,
each with one smoothly choreographed blow.

He grunts while showing his poses and paces.
His back alone has twenty different faces.
The mammoth fist he raises as he wins
is tribute to the force of vitamins.

Poetry Reading

To be a boxer, or not to be there
at all. O Muse, where are *our* teeming crowds?
Twelve people in the room, eight seats to spare —
it's time to start this cultural affair.
Half came inside because it started raining,
the rest are relatives. O Muse.

The women here would love to rant and rave,
but that's for boxing. Here they must behave.
Dante's Inferno is ringside nowadays.
Likewise his Paradise. O Muse.

Oh, not to be a boxer but a poet,
one sentenced to hard shelleying for life,
for lack of muscles forced to show the world
the sonnet that may make the high-school reading lists
with luck. O Muse,
O bobtailed angel, Pegasus.

In the first row, a sweet old man's soft snore:
he dreams his wife's alive again. What's more,
she's making him that tart she used to bake.
Aflame, but carefully — don't burn his cake! —
we start to read. O Muse.

Epitaph

Here lies, old-fashioned as parentheses,
the authoress of verse. Eternal rest
was granted her by earth, although the corpse
had failed to join the avant-garde, of course.
The plain grave? There's poetic justice in it,
this ditty-dirge, the owl, the burdock. Passerby,
take out your compact Compu-Brain and try
to weigh Szymborska's fate for half a minute.

Prologue to a Comedy

He made himself a glass violin so he could see what music looks like. He dragged his boat to the mountain's peak and waited for the sea to reach his level. At night, he got engrossed in railway schedules: the terminals moved him to tears. He grew rozes with a "z." He wrote one poem to cure baldness, and another on the same subject. He broke the clock at City Hall to stop the leaves from falling once and for all. He planned to excavate a city in a pot of chives. He walked with the globe chained to his leg, very slowly, smiling, happy as two times two is two. When they said he didn't exist, he couldn't die of grief, so he had to be born. He's already out there living somewhere; he blinks his little eyes and grows. Just in time! The very nick of time! Our Most Gracious Lady, Our Wise and Sweet Lady Machine will soon have need of a fool like this for her fit amusement and innocent pleasure.

Likeness

If the gods' favorites die young—
what to do with the rest of your life?
Old age is a precipice,
that is, if youth is a peak.

I won't budge.
I'll stay young if I have to do it on one leg.
I'll latch onto the air
with whiskers thin as a mouse's squeak.
In this posture I'll be born over and over.
It's the only art I know.

But these things will always be me:
the magic gloves,
the boutonniere left from my first masquerade,
the falsetto of youthful manifestos,
the face straight from a seamstress's dream about a croupier,
the eyes I loved to pluck out in my paintings
and scatter like peas from a pod,
because at that sight a twitch ran through the dead thighs
of the public frog.

Be amazed, you too.
Be amazed: for all of Diogenes' tubs,
I still beat him as conceptualist.
Pray
for your eternal test.
What I hold in my hands
are the spiders that I dip in Chinese ink
and fling against the canvas.
I enter the world once more.
A new navel blooms
on the artist's belly.

* * *

I am too close for him to dream of me.
I don't flutter over him, don't flee him
beneath the roots of trees. I am too close.
The caught fish doesn't sing with my voice.
The ring doesn't roll from my finger.
I am too close. The great house is on fire
without me calling for help. Too close
for one of my hairs to turn into the rope
of the alarm bell. Too close to enter
as the guest before whom walls retreat.
I'll never die again so lightly,
so far beyond my body, so unknowingly
as I did once in his dream. I am too close,
too close. I hear the word hiss
and see its glistening scales as I lie motionless
in his embrace. He's sleeping,
more accessible at this moment to an usherette
he saw once in a traveling circus with one lion
than to me, who lies at his side.
A valley now grows within him for her,
rusty-leaved, with a snowcapped mountain at one end
rising in the azure air. I am too close
to fall from that sky like a gift from heaven.

My cry could only waken him. And what
a poor gift: I, confined to my own form,
when I used to be a birch, a lizard
shedding times and satin skins
in many shimmering hues. And I possessed
the gift of vanishing before astonished eyes,
which is the richest of all. I am too close,
too close for him to dream of me.
I slip my arm from underneath his sleeping head –
it's numb, swarming with imaginary pins.
A host of fallen angels perches on each tip,
waiting to be counted.

The Tower of Babel

"*What time is it?*" "Oh yes, I'm so happy;
all I need is a little bell round my neck
to jingle over you while you're asleep."
"*Didn't you hear the storm? The north wind shook
the walls; the tower gate, like a lion's maw,
yawned on its creaking hinges.*" "How could you
forget? I had on that plain gray dress
that fastens on the shoulder." "*At that moment,
myriad explosions shook the sky.*" "How could I
come in? You weren't alone, after all." "*I glimpsed
colors older than sight itself.*" "Too bad
you can't promise me." "*You're right, it must have been
a dream.*" "Why all these lies; why do you call me
by her name; do you still love her?" "*Of course,
I want you to stay with me.*" "I can't
complain. I should have guessed myself."
"*Do you still think about him?*" "But I'm not crying."
"*That's all there is?*" "No one but you."
"*At least you're honest.*" "Don't worry,
I'm leaving town." "*Don't worry,
I'm going.*" "You have such beautiful hands."
"*That's ancient history; the blade went through
but missed the bone.*" "Never mind, darling,
never mind." "*I don't know
what time it is, and I don't care.*"

Dream

My fallen, my turned to dust, my earth,
assumes the shape he has in the photograph:
with a leaf's shadow on his face, with a seashell in his hand,
he sets out toward my dream.

He wanders through darknesses extinguished since never,
through emptinesses opened to themselves forever,
through seven times seven times seven silences.

He appears on the other side of my eyelids,
in the one and only world that he can reach.
His shot heart beats.
A first wind stirs from his hair.

A meadow unspreads between us.
Skies come flying with clouds and birds,
mountains rise silently on the horizon
and a river spurts downward, searching for the sea.

You can see so far, so far,
that day and night turn simultaneous,
and all seasons of the year occur at once.
A four-quartered moon unfolds its fan,
snowflakes swarm beside butterflies,
fruit falls from the blossoming tree.

We draw closer. In tears,
in smiles, I don't know. Just one step more
and we'll listen to your shell together,
to the roar of a thousand orchestras,
to the roar of our wedding march.

Water

A drop of water fell on my hand,
drawn from the Ganges and the Nile,

from hoarfrost ascended to heaven off a seal's whiskers,
from jugs broken in the cities of Ys and Tyre.

On my index finger
the Caspian Sea isn't landlocked,

and the Pacific is the Rudawa's meek tributary,
the same stream that floated in a little cloud over Paris

in the year seven hundred and sixty-four
on the seventh of May at three A.M.

There are not enough mouths to utter
all your fleeting names, O water.

I would have to name you in every tongue,
pronouncing all the vowels at once

while also keeping silent — for the sake of the lake
that still goes unnamed

and doesn't exist on this earth, just as the star
reflected in it is not in the sky.

Someone was drowning, someone dying was
calling out for you. Long ago, yesterday.

You have saved houses from fire, you have carried off
houses and trees, forests and towns alike.

You've been in christening fonts and courtesans' baths.
In coffins and kisses.

Gnawing at stone, feeding rainbows.
In the sweat and the dew of pyramids and lilacs.

How light the raindrop's contents are.
How gently the world touches me.

Whenever wherever whatever has happened
is written on waters of Babel.

Synopsis

Job, sorely tried in both flesh and possessions, curses man's fate. It is great poetry. His friends arrive and, rending their garments, dissect Job's guilt before the Lord. Job cries out that he was righteous. Job does not know why the Lord smote him. Job does not want to talk to them. Job wants to talk to the Lord. The Lord God appears in a chariot of whirlwinds. Before him who had been cloven to the bone, He praises the work of His hands: the heavens, the seas, the earth and the beasts thereon. Especially Behemoth, and Leviathan in particular, creatures of which the Deity is justly proud. It is great poetry. Job listens: the Lord God beats around the bush, for the Lord God wishes to beat around the bush. Job therefore hastily prostrates himself before the Lord. Events now transpire in rapid succession. Job regains his donkeys and camels, his oxen and sheep twofold. Skin grows over his grinning skull. And Job goes along with it. Job agrees. Job does not want to ruin a masterpiece.

In Heraclitus's River

In Heraclitus's river
a fish is busy fishing,
a fish guts a fish with a sharp fish,
a fish builds a fish, a fish lives in a fish,
a fish escapes from a fish under siege.

In Heraclitus's river
a fish loves a fish,
your eyes, it says, glow like the fishes in the sky,
I would swim at your side to the sea we will share,
O fairest of the shoal.

In Heraclitus's river
a fish has imagined the fish of all fish,
a fish kneels to the fish, a fish sings to the fish,
a fish begs the fish to ease its fishy lot.

In Heraclitus's river
I, the solitary fish, a fish apart
(apart at least from the tree fish and the stone fish),
write, at isolated moments, a tiny fish or two
whose glittering scales, so fleeting,
may only be the dark's embarrassed wink.

Poem in Honor

So he once was. He invented zero.
In an uncertain country. Under a star
now perhaps gone dark. Between dates
to which no one will swear. Without even
a questionable name. Without leaving
beneath his zero any pearls of wisdom
about life, which is like what. Or a legend
that one day he scribbled zero
on a plucked rose and bound it in a bouquet.
That before he died he took to the desert
on a hundred-humped camel. That he nodded off
beneath the palme d'or. That he will awaken
when everything is counted
down to the last grain of sand. What a man.
He escaped our notice through the crack
between fact and fiction. Immune
to every fate. He shakes off
every shape I give him.
Silence grew over him, without a voice's scar.
Absence mimicked the horizon.
Zero writes itself.

A Note

The first display case
holds a stone.
On it we note
a faint scratch.
A matter of chance,
some people say.

The second display case
shows a piece of frontal bone.
It cannot be proven —
is it animal or human.
Bones are bones.
Let's move on.
Nothing here.

What endures —
just the old resemblance
between a spark struck from a stone
and a star.
Severed by centuries
the space of comparison
remains the same.

The space
that lured us from the species,
led us from the sphere of sleep
before we knew the word sleep,
in which whatever lives
is born for always
and dies without death.

The space
that turned our head human,
from a spark to a star,
from one to many,
from each to all,
from temple to temple,
and that which has no eyelids
opened in us.

The sky rose
from a stone.
A stick branched
into a thicket of endings.
The snake raised its fangs
from the bundle of its reasons.
Time swirled
in the rings of a tree.
Howls of one awakened
multiplied in echoes.

The first display case
holds a stone.
The second display case
shows a piece of frontal bone.
We left the animals behind.
Who will leave us.
Through which resemblance.
What compared to what.

Conversation with a Stone

I knock at the stone's front door.
"It's only me, let me come in.
I want to enter your insides,
have a look round,
breathe my fill of you."

"Go away," says the stone.
"I'm shut tight.
Even if you break me to pieces,
we'll all still be closed.
You can grind us to sand,
we still won't let you in."

I knock at the stone's front door.
"It's only me, let me come in.
I've come out of pure curiosity.
Only life can quench it.
I mean to stroll through your palace,
then go calling on a leaf, a drop of water.
I don't have much time.
My mortality should touch you."

"I'm made of stone," says the stone,
"and must therefore keep a straight face.
Go away.
I don't have the muscles to laugh."

I knock at the stone's front door.
"It's only me, let me come in.
I hear you have great empty halls inside you,
unseen, their beauty in vain,

soundless, not echoing anyone's steps.
Admit you don't know them well yourself."

"Great and empty, true enough," says the stone,
"but there isn't any room.
Beautiful, perhaps, but not to the taste
of your poor senses.
You may get to know me, but you'll never know me through.
My whole surface is turned toward you,
all my insides turned away."

I knock at the stone's front door.
"It's only me, let me come in.
I don't seek refuge for eternity.
I'm not unhappy.
I'm not homeless.
My world is worth returning to.
I'll enter and exit empty-handed.
And my proof I was there
will be only words,
which no one will believe."

"You shall not enter," says the stone.
"You lack the sense of taking part.
No other sense can make up for your missing sense of
 taking part.
Even sight heightened to become all-seeing
will do you no good without a sense of taking part.
You shall not enter, you have only a sense of what that sense
 should be,
only its seed, imagination."

I knock at the stone's front door.
"It's only me, let me come in.
I haven't got two thousand centuries,
so let me come under your roof."

"If you don't believe me," says the stone,
"just ask the leaf, it will tell you the same.
Ask a drop of water, it will say what the leaf has said.
And, finally, ask a hair from your own head.
I am bursting with laughter, yes, laughter, vast laughter,
although I don't know how to laugh."

I knock at the stone's front door.
"It's only me, let me come in."

"I don't have a door," says the stone.

NO END OF FUN

1967

The Joy of Writing

Why does this written doe bound through these written woods?
For a drink of written water from a spring
whose surface will xerox her soft muzzle?
Why does she lift her head; does she hear something?
Perched on four slim legs borrowed from the truth,
she pricks up her ears beneath my fingertips.
Silence — this word also rustles across the page
and parts the boughs
that have sprouted from the word "woods."

Lying in wait, set to pounce on the blank page,
are letters up to no good,
clutches of clauses so subordinate
they'll never let her get away.

Each drop of ink contains a fair supply
of hunters, equipped with squinting eyes behind their sights,
prepared to swarm the sloping pen at any moment,
surround the doe, and slowly aim their guns.

They forget that what's here isn't life.
Other laws, black on white, obtain.
The twinkling of an eye will take as long as I say,
and will, if I wish, divide into tiny eternities,
full of bullets stopped in midflight.
Not a thing will ever happen unless I say so.
Without my blessing, not a leaf will fall,
not a blade of grass will bend beneath that little hoof's full stop.

Is there then a world
where I rule absolutely on fate?
A time I bind with chains of signs?
An existence become endless at my bidding?

The joy of writing.
The power of preserving.
Revenge of a mortal hand.

Memory Finally

Memory's finally found what it was after.
My mother has turned up, my father has been spotted.
I dreamed up a table and two chairs. They sat.
They were mine again, alive again for me.
The two lamps of their faces gleamed at dusk
as if for Rembrandt.

Only now can I begin to tell
in how many dreams they've wandered, in how many crowds
I dragged them out from underneath the wheels,
in how many deathbeds they moaned with me at their side.
Cut off, they grew back, but never straight.
The absurdity drove them to disguises.
So what if they felt no pain outside me,
they still ached within me.
In my dreams, gawking crowds heard me call out Mom
to a bouncing, chirping thing up on a branch.
They made fun of my father's hair in pigtails.
I woke up ashamed.

So, finally.
One ordinary Friday night
they suddenly came back
exactly as I wanted.
In a dream, but somehow freed from dreams,
obeying just themselves and nothing else.
In the picture's background possibilities grew dim,
accidents lacked the necessary shape.

Only they shone, beautiful because just like themselves.
They appeared to me for a long, long, happy time.

I woke up. I opened my eyes.
I touched the world, a chiseled picture frame.

Landscape

In the old master's landscape,
the trees have roots beneath the oil paint,
the path undoubtedly reaches its goal,
the signature is replaced by a stately blade of grass,
it's a persuasive five in the afternoon,
May has been gently, yet firmly, detained,
so I've lingered, too. Why, of course, my dear,
I am the woman there, under the ash tree.

Just see how far behind I've left you,
see the white bonnet and the yellow skirt I wear,
see how I grip my basket so as not to slip out of the painting,
how I strut within another's fate
and rest awhile from living mysteries.

Even if you called I wouldn't hear you,
and even if I heard I wouldn't turn,
and even if I made that impossible gesture
your face would seem a stranger's face to me.

I know the world six miles around.
I know the herbs and spells for every pain.
God still looks down on the crown of my head.
I still pray I won't die suddenly.
War is punishment and peace is a reward.
Shameful dreams all come from Satan.
My soul is as plain as the stone of a plum.

I don't know the games of the heart.
I've never seen my children's father naked.

I don't see the crabbed and blotted draft
that hides behind the Song of Songs.
What I want to say comes in ready-made phrases.
I never use despair, since it isn't really mine,
only given to me for safekeeping.

Even if you bar my way,
even if you stare me in the face,
I'll pass you by on the chasm's edge, finer than a hair.

On the right is my house. I know it from all sides,
along with its steps and its entryway,
behind which life goes on unpainted.
The cat hops on a bench,
the sun gleams on a pewter jug,
a bony man sits at the table
fixing a clock.

Family Album

No one in this family has ever died of love.
No food for myth and nothing magisterial.
Consumptive Romeos? Juliets diphtherial?
A doddering second childhood was enough.
No death-defying vigils, love-struck poses
over unrequited letters strewn with tears!
Here, in conclusion, as scheduled, appears
a portly, pince-nez'd neighbor bearing roses.
No suffocation-in-the-closet gaffes
because the cuckold returned home too early!
Those frills or furbelows, however flounced and whirly,
barred no one from the family photographs.
No Bosch-like hell within their souls, no wretches
found bleeding in the garden, shirts in stains!
(True, some did die with bullets in their brains,
for other reasons, though, and on field stretchers.)
Even this belle with rapturous coiffure
who may have danced till dawn—but nothing smarter—
hemorrhaged to a better world, *bien sûr,*
but not to taunt or hurt *you,* slick-haired partner.
For others, Death was mad and monumental—
not for these citizens of a sepia past.
Their griefs turned into smiles, their days flew fast,
their vanishing was due to influenza.

Laughter

The little girl I was —
I know her, of course.
I have a few snapshots
from her brief life.
I feel good-natured pity
for a couple of little poems.
I remember a few events.

But
to make the man who's with me
laugh and hug me,
I dig up just one silly story:
the puppy love
of that ugly duckling.

I tell him
how she fell in love with a college boy;
that is, she wanted him
to look at her.

I tell him
how she once ran out to meet him
with a bandage on her unhurt head,
so that he'd ask, oh just ask her
what had happened.

Funny little thing
How could she know
that even despair can work for you
if you're lucky enough
to outlive it.

I'd give her some change: go buy a cookie.
I'd give her more: go see a show.
Go away, I'm busy now.

Can't you see
the lights are out?
Don't you get it,
the door is locked?
Stop fiddling with the knob —
the man who laughed
and hugged me
is not your college boy.

It'd be better if you
went back where you came from.
I don't owe you anything,
I'm just an ordinary woman
who only knows
when to betray
another's secret.

Don't keep staring at us
with those eyes of yours,
open too wide
like the eyes of the dead.

The Railroad Station

My nonarrival in the city of N.
took place on the dot.

You'd been alerted
in my unmailed letter.

You were able not to be there
at the agreed-upon time.

The train pulled up at Platform 3.
A lot of people got out.

My absence joined the throng
as it made its way toward the exit.

Several women rushed
to take my place
in all that rush.

Somebody ran up to one of them.
I didn't know him,
but she recognized him
immediately.

While they kissed
with not our lips,
a suitcase disappeared,
not mine.

The railroad station in the city of N.
passed its exam
in objective existence
with flying colors.

The whole remained in place.
Particulars scurried
along the designated tracks.

Even a rendezvous
took place as planned.

Beyond the reach
of our presence.

In the paradise lost
of probability.

Somewhere else.
Somewhere else.
How these little words ring.

Alive

These days we just hold him.
Hold him living.
Only the heart
still pounces on him.

To the dismay
of our distaff cousin, the spider,
he will not be devoured.

We permit his head,
pardoned centuries ago,
to rest upon our shoulder.

For a thousand tangled reasons
it's become our practice
to listen to him breathe.

Hissed from our mysteries.
Broken of our bloody ways.
Stripped of female menace.

Only the fingernails
still glitter, scratch, and retract.
Do they know,
can they guess
that they're the last set of silverware
from the family fortune?

He's already forgotten
he should flee us.
He doesn't know the wide-eyed fear
that grabs you by the short hairs.

He looks as if
he'd just been born.
All out of us.
All ours.

On his cheek,
an eyelash's imploring shadow.
Between his shoulder blades,
a touching trickle of sweat.

That's what he is now,
and that's how he'll nod off.
Truthful.
Hugged by a death
whose permit has elapsed.

Born

So this is his mother.
This small woman.
The gray-eyed procreator.

The boat in which, years ago,
he sailed to shore.

The boat from which he stepped
into the world,
into un-eternity.

Genetrix of the man
with whom I leap through fire.

So this is she, the only one
who didn't take him
finished and complete.

She herself pulled him
into the skin I know,
bound him to the bones
that are hidden from me.

She herself raised
the gray eyes
that he raised to me.

So this is she, his Alpha.
Why has he shown her to me.

Born.
So he was born, too.
Born like everyone else.
Like me, who will die.

The son of an actual woman.
A new arrival from the body's depths.
A voyager to Omega.

Subject to
his own absence,
on every front,
at any moment.

He hits his head
against a wall
that won't give way forever.

His movements
dodge and parry
the universal verdict.

I realized
that his journey was already halfway over.

But he didn't tell me that,
no.

"This is my mother"
was all he said.

Census

On the hill where Troy once stood,
they've dug up seven cities.
Seven cities. Six too many
for a single epic.
What's to be done with them? What?
Hexameters burst,
nonfictional bricks appear between the cracks,
ruined walls rise mutely as in silent films,
charred beams, broken chains,
bottomless pitchers drained dry,
fertility charms, olive pits,
and skulls as palpable as tomorrow's moon.

Our stockpile of antiquity grows constantly,
it's overflowing,
reckless squatters jostle for a place in history,
hordes of sword fodder,
Hector's nameless extras, no less brave than he,
thousands upon thousands of singular faces,
each the first and last for all time,
in each a pair of inimitable eyes.
How easy it was to live not knowing this,
so sentimental, so spacious.

What should we give them? What do they need?
Some more or less unpeopled century?
Some small appreciation for their goldsmiths' art?
We three billion judges
have problems of our own,
our own inarticulate rabble,
railroad stations, bleachers, protests and processions,
vast numbers of remote streets, floors, and walls.
We pass each other once for all time in department stores
shopping for a new pitcher.
Homer is working in the census bureau.
No one knows what he does in his spare time.

Soliloquy for Cassandra

Here I am, Cassandra.
And this is my city under ashes.
And these are my prophet's staff and ribbons.
And this is my head full of doubts.

It's true, I am triumphant.
My prophetic words burn like fire in the sky.
Only unacknowledged prophets
are privy to such prospects.
Only those who got off on the wrong foot,
whose predictions turned to fact so quickly—
it's as if they'd never lived.

I remember it so clearly—
how people, seeing me, would break off in midword.
Laughter died.
Lovers' hands unclasped.
Children ran to their mothers.
I didn't even know their short-lived names.
And that song about a little green leaf—
no one ever finished it near me.

I loved them.
But I loved them haughtily.
From heights beyond life.
From the future. Where it's always empty
and nothing is easier than seeing death.
I'm sorry that my voice was hard.
Look down on yourselves from the stars, I cried,
look down on yourselves from the stars.
They heard me and lowered their eyes.

They lived within life.
Pierced by that great wind.
Condemned.
Trapped from birth in departing bodies.
But in them they bore a moist hope,
a flame fueled by its own flickering.
They really knew what a moment means,
oh any moment, any one at all
before —

It turns out I was right.
But nothing has come of it.
And this is my robe, slightly singed.
And this is my prophet's junk.
And this is my twisted face.
A face that didn't know it could be beautiful.

A Byzantine Mosaic

"O Theotropia, my empress consort."

"O Theodendron, my consort emperor."

"How fair thou art, my hollow-cheeked beloved."

"How fine art thou, blue-lipped spouse."

"Thou art so wondrous frail
beneath thy bell-like gown,
the alarum of which, if but removed,
would waken all my kingdom."

"How excellently mortified thou art,
my lord and master,
to mine own shadow a twinnèd shade."

"Oh how it pleaseth me
to see my lady's palms,
like unto palm leaves verily,
clasped to her mantle's throat."

"Wherewith, raised heavenward,
I would pray thee mercy for our son,
for he is not such as we, O Theodendron."

"Heaven forfend, O Theotropia.
Pray, what might he be,
begotten and brought forth
in godly dignity?"

"I will confess anon, and thou shalt hear me.
Not a princeling but a sinner have I borne thee.
Pink and shameless as a piglet,

plump and merry, verily,
all chubby wrists and ringlets came he
rolling unto us."

"He is roly-poly?"

"That he is."

"He is voracious?"

"Yea, in truth."

"His skin is milk and roses?"

"As thou sayest."

"What, pray, does our archimandrite say,
a man of most penetrating gnosis?
What say our consecrated eremites,
most holy skeletesses?
How should they strip the fiendish infant
of his swaddling silks?"

"Metamorphosis miraculous
still lies within our Savior's power.
Yet thou, on spying
the babe's unsightliness,
shalt not cry out
and rouse the sleeping demon from his rest?"

"I am thy twin in horror.
Lead on, Theotropia."

Beheading

Décolletage comes from *decollo,*
decollo means I cut off at the neck.
The Queen of Scots, Mary Stuart,
ascended the scaffold in an appropriate shift.
The shift was *décolleté*
and red as a hemorrhage.

At that very moment,
in a secluded chamber,
Elizabeth Tudor, Queen of England,
stood at the window in a white dress.
The dress was triumphantly fastened to the chin
and finished in a starched ruff.

They thought in unison:
"Lord, have mercy on me"
"Right is on my side"
"Living means getting in the way"
"Under certain circumstances the owl is the baker's daughter"
"This will never end"
"It is already over"
"What am I doing here, there's nothing here"

The difference in dress—yes, this we know for sure.
The detail
is unyielding.

Pietà

In the town where the hero was born you may:
gaze at the monument, admire its size,
shoo two chickens from the empty museum's steps,
ask for his mother's address,
knock, push the creaking door open.
Her bearing is erect, her hair is straight, her gaze is clear.
You may tell her that you've just arrived from Poland.
You may bear greetings. Make your questions loud and clear.
Yes, she loved him very much. Yes, he was born that way.
Yes, she was standing by the prison wall that morning.
Yes, she heard the shots.
You may regret not having brought a camera,
a tape recorder. Yes, she has seen such things.
She read his final letter on the radio.
She sang his favorite lullabies once on TV.
And once she even acted in a movie, in tears
from the bright lights. Yes, the memory still moves her.
Yes, just a little tired now. Yes, it will pass.
You may get up. Thank her. Say goodbye. Leave,
passing by the new arrivals in the hall.

Innocence

Conceived on a mattress made of human hair.
Gerda. Erika. Maybe Margarete.
She doesn't know, no, not a thing about it.
This kind of knowledge isn't suited
to being passed on or absorbed.
The Greek Furies were too righteous.
Their birdy excess would rub us the wrong way.

Irma. Brigitte. Maybe Frederika.
She's twenty-two, perhaps a little older.
She knows the three languages that all travelers need.
The company she works for plans to export
the finest mattresses, synthetic fiber only.
Trade brings nations closer.

Berta. Ulrike. Maybe Hildegard.
Not beautiful perhaps, but tall and slim.
Cheeks, neck, breasts, thighs, belly
in full bloom now, shiny and new.
Blissfully barefoot on Europe's beaches,
she unbraids her bright hair, right down to her knees.

My advice: don't cut it (her hairdresser says);
once you have, it'll never grow back so thick.
Trust me.
It's been proved
tausend- und tausendmal.

Vietnam

"Woman, what's your name?" "I don't know."
"How old are you? Where are you from?" "I don't know."
"Why did you dig that burrow?" "I don't know."
"How long have you been hiding?" "I don't know."
"Why did you bite my finger?" "I don't know."
"Don't you know that we won't hurt you?" "I don't know."
"Whose side are you on?" "I don't know."
"This is war, you've got to choose." "I don't know."
"Does your village still exist?" "I don't know."
"Are those your children?" "Yes."

Written in a Hotel

Kyoto is fortunate,
fortunate and full of palaces,
winged roofs,
stairs like musical scales.
Aged but flirtatious,
stony but alive,
wooden,
but growing from sky to earth,
Kyoto is a city
whose beauty moves you to tears.

I mean the real tears
of a certain gentleman,
a connoisseur, lover of antiquities,
who at a key moment,
from behind a green table,
exclaimed that after all
there are so many inferior cities
and burst out sobbing
in his seat.

That's how Kyoto, far lovelier
than Hiroshima, was saved.

But this is ancient history.
I can't dwell on it forever
or keep asking endlessly,
what's next, what's next.

Day to day I trust in permanence,
in history's prospects.
I can't gnaw apples
in a constant state of terror.

Now and then I hear about some Prometheus
wearing his fire helmet,
enjoying his grandkids.

While writing these lines
I wonder
what in them will come to sound
ridiculous and when.

Fear strikes me
only at times.
On the road.
In a strange city.

With garden-variety brick walls,
a tower, old and ordinary,
stucco peeling under slapdash moldings,
cracker-box housing projects,
nothing,
a helpless little tree.

What would he do here,
that tenderhearted gentleman,
the connoisseur, lover of antiquities.

Plaster god, have mercy on him.
Heave a sigh, oh classic,
from the depths of your mass-produced bust.

Only now and then,
in a city, one of many.
In a hotel room
overlooking the gutter
with a cat howling like a baby
under the stars.

In a city with lots of people,
many more than you'll find painted
on jugs, cups, saucers, and silk screens.

In a city about which I know
this one thing:
it's not Kyoto,
not Kyoto for sure.

A Film from the Sixties

This adult male. This person on earth.
Ten billion nerve cells. Ten pints of blood
pumped by ten ounces of heart.
This object took three billion years to emerge.

He first took the shape of a small boy.
The boy would lean his head on his aunt's knees.
Where is that boy. Where are those knees.
The little boy got big. Those were the days.
These mirrors are cruel and smooth as asphalt.
Yesterday he ran over a cat. Yes, not a bad idea.
The cat was saved from this age's hell.
A girl in a car checked him out.
No, her knees weren't what he's looking for.
Anyway he just wants to lie in the sand and breathe.
He has nothing in common with the world.
He feels like a handle broken off a jug,
but the jug doesn't know it's broken and keeps going to the well.
It's amazing. Someone's still willing to work.
The house gets built. The doorknob has been carved.
The tree is grafted. The circus will go on.
The whole won't go to pieces, although it's made of them.
Thick and heavy as glue *sunt lacrimae rerum.*
But all that's only background, incidental.
Within him, there's awful darkness, in the darkness a small boy.

God of humor, do something about him, OK?
God of humor, do something about him today.

Report from the Hospital

We used matches to draw lots: who would visit him.
And I lost. I got up from our table.
Visiting hours were just about to start.

When I said hello he didn't say a word.
I tried to take his hand — he pulled it back
like a hungry dog that won't give up his bone.

He seemed embarrassed about dying.
What do you say to someone like that?
Our eyes never met, like in a faked photograph.

He didn't care if I stayed or left.
He didn't ask about anyone from our table.
Not you, Barry. Or you, Larry. Or you, Harry.

My head started aching. Who's dying on whom?
I went on about modern medicine and the three violets in a jar.
I talked about the sun and faded out.

It's a good thing they have stairs to run down.
It's a good thing they have gates to let you out.
It's a good thing you're all waiting at our table.

The hospital smell makes me sick.

Returning Birds

This spring the birds came back again too early.
Rejoice, O reason: instinct can err, too.
It gathers wool, it dozes off—and down they fall
into the snow, into a foolish fate, a death
that doesn't suit their well-wrought throats and splendid claws,
their honest cartilage and conscientious webbing,
the heart's sensible sluice, the entrails' maze,
the nave of ribs, the vertebrae in stunning enfilades,
feathers deserving their own wing in any crafts museum,
the Benedictine patience of the beak.

This is not a dirge—no, it's only indignation.
An angel made of earthbound protein,
a living kite with glands straight from the Song of Songs,
singular in air, without number in the hand,
its tissues tied into a common knot
of place and time, as in an Aristotelian drama
unfolding to the wings' applause,
falls down and lies beside a stone,
which in its own archaic, simpleminded way
sees life as a chain of failed attempts.

Thomas Mann

Dear mermaids, it was bound to happen.
Beloved fauns and honorable angels,
evolution has emphatically cast you out.
Not that it lacks imagination, but
you with your Devonian tail fins and alluvial breasts,
your fingered hands and cloven feet,
your arms alongside, not instead of, wings,
your, heaven help us, diphyletic skeletons,
your ill-timed tails, horns sprouted out of spite,
illegitimate beaks, this morphogenetic potpourri, those
finned or furry frills and furbelows, the couplets
pairing human/heron with such cunning
that their offspring knows all, is immortal, and can fly,
you must admit that it would be a nasty joke,
excessive, everlasting, and no end of bother,
one that mother nature wouldn't like and won't allow.

And after all she does permit a fish to fly,
deft and defiant. Each such ascent
consoles our rule-bound world, reprieves it
from necessity's confines — more
than enough for the world to be a world.

And after all she does permit us baroque gems
like this: a platypus that feeds its chicks on milk.
She might have said no — and which of us would know
that we'd been robbed?

But the best is that
she somehow missed the moment when a mammal turned up
with its hand miraculously feathered by a fountain pen.

Tarsier

I am a tarsier and a tarsier's son,
the grandson and great-grandson of tarsiers,
a tiny creature, made up of two pupils
and whatever simply could not be left out;
miraculously saved from further alterations —
since I'm no one's idea of a treat,
my coat's too small for a fur collar,
my glands provide no bliss,
and concerts go on without my gut —
I, a tarsier,
sit living on a human fingertip.

Good morning, lord and master,
what will you give me
for not taking anything from me?
How will you reward me for your own magnanimity?
What price will you set on my priceless head
for the poses I strike to make you smile?

My good lord is gracious,
my good lord is kind.
Who else could bear such witness if there were
no creatures unworthy of death?
You yourselves, perhaps?
But what you've come to know about yourselves
will serve for a sleepless night from star to star.

And only we few who remain unstripped of fur,
untorn from bone, unplucked of soaring feathers,
esteemed in all our quills, scales, tusks, and horns,
and in whatever else that ingenious protein

has seen fit to clothe us with,
we, my lord, are your dream,
which finds you innocent for now.

I am a tarsier — the father and grandfather of tarsiers —
a tiny creature, nearly half of something,
yet nonetheless a whole no less than others,
so light that twigs spring up beneath my weight
and might have lifted me to heaven long ago
if I hadn't had to fall
time and again
like a stone lifted from hearts
grown oh so sentimental:
I, a tarsier,
know well how essential it is to be a tarsier.

To My Heart, on Sunday

Thank you, my heart:
you don't dawdle, you keep going
with no flattery or reward,
just from inborn diligence.

You get seventy credits a minute.
Each of your systoles
shoves a little boat
to open sea
to sail around the world.

Thank you, my heart:
time after time
you pluck me, separate even in sleep,
out of the whole.

You make sure I don't dream my dreams
up to that final flight,
no wings required.

Thank you, my heart:
I woke up again
and even though it's Sunday,
the day of rest,
the usual preholiday rush
continues underneath my ribs.

The Acrobat

From trapeze to
to trapeze, in the hush that
that follows the drum roll's sudden pause, through
through the startled air, more swiftly than
than his body's weight, which once again
again is late for its own fall.

Solo. Or even less than solo,
less, because he's crippled, missing
missing wings, missing them so much
that he can't miss the chance
to soar on shamefully unfeathered
naked vigilance alone.

Arduous ease,
watchful agility,
and calculated inspiration. Do you see
how he waits to pounce in flight; do you know
how he plots from head to toe
against his very being; do you know, do you see
how cunningly he weaves himself through his own former shape
and works to seize this swaying world
by stretching out the arms he has conceived—

beautiful beyond belief at this passing
at this very passing moment that's just passed.

A Paleolithic Fertility Fetish

The Great Mother has no face.
Why would the Great Mother need a face.
The face cannot stay faithful to the body,
the face disturbs the body, it is undivine,
it disturbs the body's solemn unity.
The Great Mother's visage is her bulging belly
with its blind navel in the middle.

The Great Mother has no feet.
What would the Great Mother do with feet.
Where is she going to go.
Why would she go into the world's details.
She has gone just as far as she wants
and keeps watch in the workshops under her taut skin.

So there's a world out there? Well and good.
It's bountiful? Even better.
The children have somewhere to go, to run around,
something to look up to? Wonderful.
So much that it's still there while they're sleeping,
almost ridiculously whole and real?
It keeps on existing when their backs are turned?
That's just too much – it shouldn't have.

The Great Mother barely has a pair of arms,
two tiny limbs lie lazing on her breasts.
Why would they want to bless life,
give gifts to what has enough and more!

Their only obligation is to endure as long as earth and sky
just in case
of some mishap that never comes.
To form a zigzag over essence.
The ornament's last laugh.

Cave

There's nothing on the walls
except for dampness.
It's cold and dark in here.

But cold and dark
after a burnt-out fire.
Nothing, but nothing remaining
from a bison drawn in ocher.

Nothing—but a nothing left
after the long resistance
of the beast's lowered brow.
So, a Beautiful Nothing.
Deserving a capital letter.
A heresy against humdrum nothingness,
unconverted and proud of the difference.

Nothing—but after us,
who were here before
and ate our hearts
and drank our blood.

Nothing, to wit:
our unfinished dance.
Your first thighs, arms, necks, faces
by the fire.
My first sacred bellies
filled with minuscule Pascals.

Silence, but after voices.
Not a sluggish sort of silence.
A silence that had its own throats once,
its flutes and tambourines.
Grafted here like a wilding
by laughter and howls.

Motion

You're crying here, but there they're dancing,
there they're dancing in your tear.
There they're happy, making merry,
they don't know a blessed thing.
Almost the glimmering of mirrors.
Almost candles flickering.
Nearly staircases and hallways.
Gestures, lace cuffs, so it seems.
Hydrogen, oxygen, those rascals.
Chlorine, sodium, a pair of rogues.
The fop nitrogen parading
up and down, around, about
beneath the vault, inside the dome.
Your crying's music to their ears.
Yes, *eine kleine Nachtmusik.*
Who are you, lovely masquerader.

No End of Fun

So he's got to have happiness,
he's got to have truth, too,
he's got to have eternity—
did you ever!

He has only just learned to tell dreams from waking;
only just realized that he is he;
only just whittled with his hand né fin
a flint, a rocket ship;
easily drowned in the ocean's teaspoon,
not even funny enough to tickle the void;
sees only with his eyes;
hears only with his ears;
his speech's personal best is the conditional;
he uses his reason to pick holes in reason.
In short, he's next to no one,
but his head's full of freedom, omniscience, and the Being
beyond his foolish meat—
did you ever!

For he does apparently exist.
He genuinely came to be
beneath one of the more parochial stars.
He's lively and quite active in his fashion.
His capacity for wonder is well advanced
for a crystal's deviant descendant.
And considering his difficult childhood
spent kowtowing to the herd's needs,
he's already quite an individual indeed—
did you ever!

Carry on, then, if only for the moment
that it takes a tiny galaxy to blink!
One wonders what will become of him,
since he does in fact seem to be.
And as far as being goes, he really tries quite hard.
Quite hard indeed — one must admit.
With that ring in his nose, with that toga, that sweater.
He's no end of fun, for all you say.
Poor little beggar.
A human, if ever we saw one.

COULD HAVE

1972

Could Have

It could have happened.
It had to happen.
It happened earlier. Later.
Nearer. Farther off.
It happened, but not to you.

You were saved because you were the first.
You were saved because you were the last.
Alone. With others.
On the right. The left.
Because it was raining. Because of the shade.
Because the day was sunny.

You were in luck—there was a forest.
You were in luck—there were no trees.
You were in luck—a rake, a hook, a beam, a brake,
a jamb, a turn, a quarter inch, an instant.
You were in luck—just then a straw went floating by.

As a result, because, although, despite.
What would have happened if a hand, a foot,
within an inch, a hairsbreadth from
an unfortunate coincidence.

So you're here? Still dizzy from another dodge,
    close shave, reprieve?
One hole in the net and you slipped through?
I couldn't be more shocked or speechless.
Listen,
how your heart pounds inside me.

Falling from the Sky

Magic is dying out, although the heights
still pulse with its vast force. On August nights
you can't be sure what's falling from the sky:
a star? or something else that still belongs on high?
Is making wishes an old-fashioned blunder
if heaven only knows what we are under?
Above our modern heads the dark's still dark,
but can't some twinkle in it explain: "I'm a spark,
I swear, a flash that a comet shook loose
from its tail, just a bit of cosmic rubble;
it's not me falling in tomorrow's news,
that's some other spark nearby, having engine trouble."

Wrong Number

At midnight, in an empty, hushed art gallery
a tactless telephone spews forth a stream of rings;
a human sleeping now would jump up instantly,
but only sleepless prophets and untiring kings
reside here, where the moonlight makes them pale;
they hold their breath, their eyes fixed on some nail
or crack; only the young pawnbroker's bride
seems taken by that odd, ringing contraption,
but even she won't lay her fan aside,
she too just hangs there, caught in mid-nonaction.
Above it all, in scarlet robes or nude,
they view nocturnal fuss as simply rude.
Here's more black humor worthy of the name
than if some grand duke leaned out from his frame
and vented his frustration with a vulgar curse.
And if some silly man calling from town
refuses to give up, put the receiver down,
though he's got the wrong number? He lives, so he errs.

Theater Impressions

For me the tragedy's most important act is the sixth:
the raising of the dead from the stage's battlegrounds,
the straightening of wigs and fancy gowns,
removing knives from stricken breasts,
taking nooses from lifeless necks,
lining up among the living
to face the audience.

The bows, both solo and ensemble —
the pale hand on the wounded heart,
the curtsies of the hapless suicide,
the bobbing of the chopped-off head.

The bows in pairs —
rage extends its arm to meekness,
the victim's eyes smile at the torturer,
the rebel indulgently walks beside the tyrant.

Eternity trampled by the golden slipper's toe.
Redeeming values swept aside with the swish of a
    wide-brimmed hat.
The unrepentant urge to start all over tomorrow.

Now enter, single file, the hosts who died early on,
in Acts 3 and 4, or between scenes.
The miraculous return of all those lost without a trace.

The thought that they've been waiting patiently offstage
without taking off their makeup
or their costumes
moves me more than all the tragedy's tirades.

But the curtain's fall is the most uplifting part,
the things you see before it hits the floor:
here one hand quickly reaches for a flower,
there another hand picks up a fallen sword.
Only then, one last, unseen, hand
does its duty
and grabs me by the throat.

Voices

You can't move an inch, my dear Marcus Emilius,
without Aborigines sprouting up as if from the earth itself.

Your heel sticks fast amidst Rutulians.
You founder knee-deep in Sabines and Latins.
You're up to your waist, your neck, your nostrils
in Aequians and Volscians, dear Lucius Fabius.

These irksome little nations, thick as flies.
It's enough to make you sick, dear Quintus Decius.

One town, then the next, then the hundred and seventieth.
The Fidenates' stubbornness. The Feliscans' ill will.
The shortsighted Ecetrans. The capricious Antemnates.
The Labicanians and Pelignians, offensively aloof.
They drive us mild-mannered sorts to sterner measures
with every new mountain we cross, dear Gaius Cloelius.

If only they weren't always in the way, the Auruncians,
    the Marsians,
but they always do get in the way, dear Spurius Manlius.

Tarquinians where you'd least expect them, Etruscans on all sides.
If that weren't enough, Volsinians and Veientians.
The Aulertians, beyond all reason. And, of course,
the endlessly vexatious Sapinians, my dear Sextus Oppius.

Little nations do have little minds.
The circle of thick skulls expands around us.
Reprehensible customs. Backward laws.
Ineffectual gods, my dear Titus Vilius.

Heaps of Hernicians. Swarms of Murricinians.
Antlike multitudes of Vestians and Samnites.
The farther you go, the more there are, dear Servius Follius.

These little nations are pitiful indeed.
Their foolish ways require supervision
with every new river we ford, dear Aulus Iunius.

Every new horizon threatens me.
That's how I'd put it, my dear Hostius Melius.

To which I, Hostius Melius, would reply, my dear
Appius Papius: March on! The world has got to end somewhere.

The Letters of the Dead

We read the letters of the dead like helpless gods,
but gods nonetheless, since we know the dates that follow.
We know which debts will never be repaid.
Which widows will remarry with the corpse still warm.
Poor dead, blindfolded dead,
gullible, fallible, pathetically prudent.
We see the faces people make behind their backs.
We catch the sound of wills being ripped to shreds.
The dead sit before us comically, as if on buttered bread,
or frantically pursue the hats blown from their heads.
Their bad taste, Napoleon, steam, electricity,
their fatal remedies for curable diseases,
their foolish apocalypse according to Saint John,
their counterfeit heaven on earth according to Jean-Jacques . . .
We watch the pawns on their chessboards in silence,
even though we see them three squares later.
Everything the dead predicted has turned out completely
 different.
Or a little bit different — which is to say, completely different.
The most fervent of them gaze confidingly into our eyes:
their calculations tell them that they'll find perfection there.

Old Folks' Home

Here comes Her Highness — well, you know who I mean,
our Helen the snooty — now who made her queen!
With her lipstick and wig on, as if we could care,
like her three sons in heaven can see her from there!

"I wouldn't be here if they'd lived through the war.
I'd spend winter with one son, summer with another."
What makes her so sure?
I'd be dead too now, with her for a mother.

And she keeps on asking ("I don't mean to pry")
why from your sons and daughters there's never a word
even though they weren't killed. "If my boys were alive,
I'd spend all my holidays home with the third."

Right, and in his gold carriage he'd come and get her,
drawn by a swan or a lily-white dove,
to show all of us that he'll never forget her
and how much he owes to her motherly love.

Even Jane herself, the nurse, can't help but grin
when our Helen starts singing this old song again —
even though Jane's job is commiseration
Monday through Friday, with two weeks' vacation.

Advertisement

I'm a tranquilizer.
I'm effective at home.
I work in the office.
I can take exams
or the witness stand.
I mend broken cups with care.
All you have to do is take me,
let me melt beneath your tongue,
just gulp me
with a glass of water.

I know how to handle misfortune,
how to take bad news.
I can minimize injustice,
lighten up God's absence,
or pick the widow's veil that suits your face.
What are you waiting for—
have faith in my chemical compassion.

You're still a young man/woman.
It's not too late to learn how to unwind.
Who said
you have to take it on the chin?

Let me have your abyss.
I'll cushion it with sleep.
You'll thank me for giving you
four paws to fall on.

Sell me your soul.
There are no other takers.

There is no other devil anymore.

Lazarus Takes a Walk

The professor has died three times now.
After the first death, he was taught to move his head.
After the second, he learned how to sit up.
After the third, they even got him on his feet,
propped up by a sturdy, chubby nanny:
Let's take a little walk, shall we, professor?

Severe brain damage following the accident
and yet—will wonders never cease—he's come so far:
left right, light dark, tree grass, hurt eat.

Two plus two, professor?
Two, says the professor.
At least he's getting warm.

Hurt, grass, sit, bench.
But at the garden's edge, that old bird,
neither pink nor cheery,
chased away three times now,
his real nanny. Or so she says—who knows?

He wants to go to her. Another tantrum.
What a shame. This time he came so close.

Snapshot of a Crowd

In the snapshot of a crowd,
my head's seventh from the edge,
or maybe fourth from the left,
or twenty-eighth from the bottom;

my head is I don't know which,
no longer on its own shoulders,
just like the rest (and vice versa),
neither clearly male nor female;

whatever it signifies
is of no significance,

and the Spirit of the Age
may just glance its way, at best;

my head is statistical,
it consumes its steel per capita
globally and with composure;

shamelessly predictable,
complacently replaceable;

as if I didn't even own it
in my own and separate way;

as if it were one skull of many
found unnamed in strip-mined graveyards
and preserved so well that one
forgets that its owner's gone;

as if it were already there,
my head, any-, everyone's —

where its memories, if any,
must reach deep into the future.

Going Home

He came home. Said nothing.
It was clear, though, that something had gone wrong.
He lay down fully dressed.
Pulled the blanket over his head.
Tucked up his knees.
He's nearly forty, but not at the moment.
He exists just as he did inside his mother's womb,
clad in seven walls of skin, in sheltered darkness.
Tomorrow he'll give a lecture
on homeostasis in megagalactic cosmonautics.
For now, though, he has curled up and gone to sleep.

Discovery

I believe in the great discovery.
I believe in the man who will make the discovery.
I believe in the fear of the man who will make the discovery.

I believe in his face going white,
his queasiness, his upper lip drenched in cold sweat.

I believe in the burning of his notes,
burning them into ashes,
burning them to the last scrap.

I believe in the scattering of numbers,
scattering them without regret.

I believe in the man's haste,
in the precision of his movements,
in his free will.

I believe in the shattering of tablets,
the pouring out of liquids,
the extinguishing of rays.

I am convinced this will end well,
that it will not be too late,
that it will take place without witnesses.

I'm sure no one will find out what happened,
not the wife, not the wall,
not even the bird that might squeal in its song.

I believe in the refusal to take part.
I believe in the ruined career.
I believe in the wasted years of work.
I believe in the secret taken to the grave.

These words soar for me beyond all rules
without seeking support from actual examples.
My faith is strong, blind, and without foundation.

Dinosaur Skeleton

Beloved Brethren,
we have before us an example of incorrect proportions.
Behold! the dinosaur's skeleton looms above—

Dear Friends,
on the left we see the tail trailing into one infinity,
on the right, the neck juts into another—

Esteemed Comrades,
in between, four legs that finally mired in the slime
beneath this hillock of a trunk—

Gentle Citizens,
nature does not err, but it loves its little joke:
please note the laughably small head—

Ladies, Gentlemen,
a head this size does not have room for foresight,
and that is why its owner is extinct—

Honored Dignitaries,
a mind too small, an appetite too large,
more senseless sleep than prudent apprehension—

Distinguished Guests,
we're in far better shape in this regard,
life is beautiful and the world is ours—

Venerated Delegation,
the starry sky above the thinking reed
and moral law within it —

Most Reverend Deputation,
such success does not come twice
and perhaps beneath this single sun alone —

Inestimable Council,
how deft the hands,
how eloquent the lips,
what a head on these shoulders —

Supremest of Courts,
so much responsibility in place of a vanished tail —

Pursuit

I know I'll be greeted by silence, but still.
No uproar, no fanfare, no applause, but still.
No alarm bells, and nothing alarming.

I don't expect even a shriveled leaf,
to say nothing of silver palaces and gardens,
venerable elders, righteous laws,
wisdom in crystal balls, but still.

I understand that I don't walk the moon
in search of ladies' rings and vanished ribbons.
They pick everything up in advance.

Nothing left to suggest that . . .
Trash, castoffs, peelings, scraps, crumbs,
chips, shavings, shards, bits, pieces.

Of course I only bend over a pebble
that bears no hint of where they've gone.
They don't like leaving signs.
They're peerless in the art of erasing traces.

I've known it for ages: the gift of vanishing just in time,
their divine ungraspability by horns or tail,
by the hem of a robe ballooning in flight.
A hair never falls from their heads that I might snatch.

They're always one thought smarter,
one step ahead, I can never catch up,
they let me play at being first.

They aren't there, they never were, but still
I have to keep telling myself,
don't be a child, stop seeing things.

And whatever just hopped from underfoot
didn't get far, it toppled over, trampled,
and though it stirs again
and emits a long-drawn muteness,
it's a shadow — too much my own to point the way.

A Speech at the Lost-and-Found

I lost a few goddesses while moving south to north,
and also some gods while moving east to west.
I let several stars go out for good, they can't be traced.
An island or two sank on me, they're lost at sea.
I'm not even sure exactly where I left my claws,
who's got my fur coat, who's living in my shell.
My siblings died the day I left for dry land
and only one small bone recalls that anniversary in me.
I've shed my skin, squandered vertebrae and legs,
taken leave of my senses time and again.
I've long since closed my third eye to all that,
washed my fins of it and shrugged my branches.

Gone, lost, scattered to the four winds. It still surprises me
how little now remains, one first person sing., temporarily
declined in human form, just now making such a fuss
about a blue umbrella left yesterday on a bus.

Astonishment

Why, after all, this one and not the rest?
Why this specific self, not in a nest,
but a house? Sewn up not in scales, but skin?
Not topped off by a leaf, but by a face?
Why on earth now, on Tuesday of all days,
and why on earth, pinned down by this star's pin?
In spite of years of my not being here?
In spite of seas of all these dates and fates,
these cells, celestials, and coelenterates?
What is it really that made me appear
neither an inch nor half a globe too far,
neither a minute nor eons too early?
What made me fill myself with me so squarely?
Why am I staring now into the dark
and muttering this unending monologue
just like the growling thing we call a dog?

Birthday

So much world all at once — how it rustles and bustles!
Moraines and morays and morasses and mussels,
the flame, the flamingo, the flounder, the feather —
how to line them all up, how to put them together?
All the thickets and crickets and creepers and creeks!
The beeches and leeches alone could take weeks.
Chinchillas, gorillas, and sarsaparillas —
thanks so much, but all this excess of kindness could kill us.
Where's the jar for this burgeoning burdock, brooks' babble,
rooks' squabble, snakes' squiggle, abundance, and trouble?
How to plug up the gold mines and pin down the fox,
how to cope with the lynx, bobolinks, streptococs!
Take dioxide: a lightweight, but mighty in deeds;
what about octopodes, what about centipedes?
I could look into prices, but don't have the nerve:
these are products I just can't afford, don't deserve.
Isn't sunset a little too much for two eyes
that, who knows, may not open to see the sun rise?
I am just passing through, it's a five-minute stop.
I won't catch what is distant; what's too close, I'll mix up.
While trying to plumb what the void's inner sense is,
I'm bound to pass by all these poppies and pansies.
What a loss when you think how much effort was spent
perfecting this petal, this pistil, this scent
for the one-time appearance, which is all they're allowed,
so aloofly precise and so fragilely proud.

Interview with a Child

The Master hasn't been among us long.
That's why he lies in wait in every corner.
Covers his eyes and peeks through the cracks.
Faces the wall, then suddenly turns around.

The Master rejects outright the ridiculous thought
that a table out of sight goes on being a table nonstop,
that a chair behind our backs stays stuck in chairlike bounds
and doesn't even try to fly the coop.

True, it's hard to catch the world being different.
The apple tree slips back under the window before you can blink.
Incandescent sparrows always grow dim just in time.
Little pitchers have big ears and pick up every sound.
The nighttime closet acts as dull as its daytime twin.
The drawer does its best to assure the Master
it holds only what it's been given.
And no matter how fast you open the Brothers Grimm,
the princess always manages to take her seat again.

"They sense I'm a stranger here," the Master sighs,
"they won't let a new kid play their private games."

Since how can it be that whatever exists
can only exist in one way,
an awful situation, for there's no escaping yourself,
no pause, no transformation? In a humble from-here-to-here?
A fly caught in a fly? A mouse trapped in a mouse?
A dog never let off its latent chain?
A fire that can't come up with anything better
than burning the Master's trustful finger one more time?

Is this the definitive, actual world:
scattered wealth that can't be gathered,
useless luxury, forbidden options?

"No," the Master cries, and stomps all the feet
he can muster — for such great despair
that beetle's six legs wouldn't be enough.

Allegro ma Non Troppo

Life, you're beautiful (I say),
you just couldn't get more fecund,
more befrogged or nightingaley,
more anthillful or sproutspouting.

I'm trying to court life's favor,
to get into its good graces,
to anticipate its whims.
I'm always the first to bow,

always there where it can see me
with my humble, reverent face,
soaring on the wings of rapture,
falling under waves of wonder.

Oh how grassy is this hopper,
how this berry ripely rasps.
I would never have conceived it
if I weren't conceived myself!

Life (I say), I've no idea
what I could compare you to.
No one else can make a pine cone
and then make the pine cone's clone.

I praise your inventiveness,
bounty, sweep, exactitude,
sense of order – gifts that border
on witchcraft and wizardry.

I just don't want to upset you,
tease or anger, vex or rile.
For millennia, I've been trying
to appease you with my smile.

I tug at life by its leaf hem:
will it stop for me, just once,
momentarily forgetting
to what end it runs and runs?

Autotomy

In danger, the holothurian cuts itself in two.
It abandons one self to a hungry world
and with the other self it flees.

It violently divides into doom and salvation,
retribution and reward, what has been and what will be.

An abyss appears in the middle of its body
between what instantly become two foreign shores.

Life on one shore, death on the other.
Here hope and there despair.

If there are scales, the pans don't move.
If there is justice, this is it.

To die just as required, without excess.
To grow back just what's needed from what's left.

We, too, can divide ourselves, it's true.
But only into flesh and a broken whisper.
Into flesh and poetry.

The throat on one side, laughter on the other,
quiet, quickly dying out.

Here the heavy heart, there *non omnis moriar*—
just three little words, like a flight's three feathers.

The abyss doesn't divide us.
The abyss surrounds us.

—*In memoriam Halina Poświatowska*

Frozen Motion

This isn't Miss Duncan, the noted danseuse?
Not the drifting cloud, the wafting zephyr, the bacchante,
moonlit waters, waves swaying, breezes sighing?

Standing this way, in the photographer's atelier,
heftily, fleshily wrested from music and motion,
she's cast to the mercies of a pose,
forced to bear false witness.

Thick arms raised above her head,
a knotted knee protrudes from her short tunic,
left leg forward, naked foot and toes,
with 5 (count them) toenails.

One short step from eternal art into artificial eternity—
I reluctantly admit that it's better than nothing
and more fitting than otherwise.

Behind the screen, a pink corset, a handbag,
in it a ticket for a steamship
leaving tomorrow, that is, sixty years ago;
never again, but still at nine A.M. sharp.

Certainty

"Thou art certain, then, our ship hath touch'd upon*
the deserts of Bohemia?" "Aye, my lord." The quote's
from Shakespeare, who, I'm certain, wasn't someone else.
Some facts and dates, a portrait nearly done before
his death . . . Who needs more? Why expect to see
the proof, snatched up once by the Greater Sea,
then cast upon this world's Bohemian shore?

* Changed from Shakespeare's "perfect." (*Translators' note*)

The Classic

A few clods of dirt, and his life will be forgotten.
The music will break free from circumstance.
No more coughing of the maestro over minuets.
Poultices will be torn off.
Fire will consume the dusty, lice-ridden wig.
Ink spots will vanish from the lace cuff.
The shoes, inconvenient witnesses, will be tossed on the
    trash heap.
The least gifted of his pupils will get the violin.
Butchers' bills will be removed from between the music sheets.
His poor mother's letters will line the stomachs of mice.
The ill-fated love will fade away.
Eyes will stop shedding tears.
The neighbors' daughter will find a use for the pink ribbon.
The age, thank God, isn't Romantic yet.
Everything that's not a quartet
will become a forgettable fifth.
Everything that's not a quintet
will become a superfluous sixth.
Everything that's not a choir made of forty angels
will fall silent, reduced to barking dogs, a gendarme's belch.
The aloe plant will be taken from the window
along with a dish of fly poison and the pomade pot,
and the view of the garden (oh yes!) will be revealed—
the garden that was never here.
Now hark! ye mortals, listen, listen now,
take heed, in rapt amazement,
O rapt, O stunned, O heedful mortals, listen,
O listeners—now listen—be all ears—

In Praise of Dreams

In my dreams
I paint like Vermeer van Delft.

I speak fluent Greek
and not just with the living.

I drive a car
that does what I want it to.

I am gifted
and write mighty epics.

I hear voices
as clearly as any venerable saint.

My brilliance as a pianist
would stun you.

I fly the way we ought to,
i.e., on my own.

Falling from the roof,
I tumble gently to the grass.

I've got no problem
breathing under water.

I can't complain:
I've been able to locate Atlantis.

It's gratifying that I can always
wake up before dying.

As soon as war breaks out,
I roll over on my other side.

I'm a child of my age,
but I don't have to be.

A few years ago
I saw two suns.

And the night before last a penguin,
clear as day.

True Love

True love. Is it normal,
is it serious, is it practical?
What does the world get from two people
who exist in a world of their own?

Placed on the same pedestal for no good reason,
drawn randomly from millions, but convinced
it had to happen this way — in reward for what? For nothing.
The light descends from nowhere.
Why on these two and not on others?
Doesn't this outrage justice? Yes it does.
Doesn't it disrupt our painstakingly erected principles,
and cast the moral from the peak? Yes on both accounts.

Look at the happy couple.
Couldn't they at least try to hide it,
fake a little depression for their friends' sake!
Listen to them laughing — it's an insult.
The language they use — deceptively clear.
And their little celebrations, rituals,
the elaborate mutual routines —
it's obviously a plot behind the human race's back!

It's hard even to guess how far things might go
if people start to follow their example.
What could religion and poetry count on?
What would be remembered? what renounced?
Who'd want to stay within bounds?

True love. Is it really necessary?
Tact and common sense tell us to pass over it in silence,
like a scandal in Life's highest circles.
Perfectly good children are born without its help.
It couldn't populate the planet in a million years,
it comes along so rarely.

Let the people who never find true love
keep saying that there's no such thing.

Their faith will make it easier for them to live and die.

* * *

Nothingness unseamed itself for me too.
It turned itself wrong side out.
How on earth did I end up here —
head to toe among the planets,
without a clue how I used not to be.

O you, encountered here and loved here,
I can only guess, my arm on yours,
how much vacancy on that side went to make us,
how much silence there for one lone cricket here,
how much nonmeadow for a single sprig of sorrel,
and sun after darknesses in a drop of dew
as repayment — for what boundless droughts?

Starry willy-nilly! Local in reverse!
Stretched out in curvatures, weights, roughnesses, and motions!
Time out from infinity for endless sky!
Relief from nonspace in a shivering birch tree's shape!

Now or never wind will stir a cloud,
since wind is exactly what won't blow there.
And a beetle hits the trail in a witness's dark suit,
testifying to the long wait for a short life.

And it so happened that I'm here with you.
And I really see nothing
usual in that.

Under One Small Star

My apologies to chance for calling it necessity.
My apologies to necessity if I'm mistaken, after all.
Please, don't be angry, happiness, that I take you as my due.
May my dead be patient with the way my memories fade.
My apologies to time for all the world I overlook each second.
My apologies to past loves for thinking that the latest is the first.
Forgive me, distant wars, for bringing flowers home.
Forgive me, open wounds, for pricking my finger.
I apologize for my record of minuets to those who cry from
the depths.
I apologize to those who wait in railway stations for being asleep
today at five A.M.
Pardon me, hounded hope, for laughing from time to time.
Pardon me, deserts, that I don't rush to you bearing a spoonful
of water.
And you, falcon, unchanging year after year, always in the
same cage,
your gaze always fixed on the same point in space,
forgive me, even if it turns out you were stuffed.
My apologies to the felled tree for the table's four legs.
My apologies to great questions for small answers.
Truth, please don't pay me much attention.
Dignity, please be magnanimous.
Bear with me, O mystery of existence, as I pluck the occasional
thread from your train.

Soul, don't take offense that I've only got you now and then.
My apologies to everything that I can't be everywhere at once.
My apologies to everyone that I can't be each woman and
each man.
I know I won't be justified as long as I live,
since I myself stand in my own way.
Don't bear me ill will, speech, that I borrow weighty words,
then labor heavily so that they may seem light.

A LARGE NUMBER

1976

A Large Number

Four billion people on this earth,
but my imagination is still the same.
It's bad with large numbers.
It's still taken by particularity.
It flits in the dark like a flashlight,
illuminating only random faces
while all the rest go blindly by,
never coming to mind and never really missed.
But even a Dante couldn't get it right.
Let alone someone who is not.
Even with all the muses behind me.

Non omnis moriar — a premature worry.
But am I entirely alive and is that enough.
It never was, and now less than ever.
My choices are rejections, since there is no other way,
but what I reject is more numerous,
denser, more demanding than before.
A little poem, a sigh, at the cost of indescribable losses.
I whisper my reply to my stentorian calling.
I can't tell you how much I pass over in silence.
A mouse at the foot of the maternal mountain.
Life lasts as long as a few signs scratched by a claw in the sand.

My dreams — even they're not as populous as they should be.
They hold more solitude than noisy crowds.
Sometimes a long-dead friend stops by awhile.
A single hand turns the knob.

An echo's annexes overgrow the empty house.
I run from the doorstep into a valley
that is quiet, as if no one owned it, already an anachronism.

Why there's still all this space inside me
I don't know.

Thank-You Note

I owe so much
to those I don't love.

The relief as I agree
that someone else needs them more.

The happiness that I'm not
the wolf to their sheep.

The peace I feel with them,
the freedom –
love can neither give
nor take that.

I don't wait for them,
as in window-to-door-and-back.
Almost as patient
as a sundial,
I understand
what love can't,
and forgive
as love never would.

From a rendezvous to a letter
is just a few days or weeks,
not an eternity.

Trips with them always go smoothly,
concerts are heard,
cathedrals visited,
scenery is seen.

And when seven hills and rivers
come between us,
the hills and rivers
can be found on any map.

They deserve the credit
if I live in three dimensions,
in nonlyrical and nonrhetorical space
with a genuine, shifting horizon.

They themselves don't realize
how much they hold in their empty hands.

"I don't owe them a thing"
would be love's answer
to this open question.

Psalm

Oh, the leaky boundaries of man-made states!
How many clouds float past them with impunity;
how much desert sand shifts from one land to another;
how many mountain pebbles tumble onto foreign soil
in provocative hops!

Need I mention every single bird that flies in the face of frontiers
or alights on the roadblock at the border?
A humble robin — still, its tail resides abroad
while its beak stays home. If that weren't enough, it won't stop
  bobbing!

Among innumerable insects, I'll single out only the ant
between the border guard's left and right boots
blithely ignoring the questions "Where from?" and "Where to?"

Oh, to register in detail, at a glance, the chaos
prevailing on every continent!
Isn't that a privet on the far bank
smuggling its hundred-thousandth leaf across the river?
And who but the octopus, with impudent long arms,
would disrupt the sacred bounds of territorial waters?

And how can we talk of order overall
when the very placement of the stars
leaves us doubting just what shines for whom?

Not to speak of the fog's reprehensible drifting!
And dust blowing all over the steppes
as if they hadn't been partitioned!
And the voices coasting on obliging airwaves,
that conspiratorial squeaking, those indecipherable mutters!

Only what is human can truly be foreign.
The rest is mixed vegetation, subversive moles, and wind.

Lot's Wife

They say I looked back out of curiosity.
But I could have had other reasons.
I looked back mourning my silver bowl.
Carelessly, while tying my sandal strap.
So I wouldn't have to keep staring at the righteous nape
of my husband Lot's neck.
From the sudden conviction that if I dropped dead
he wouldn't so much as hesitate.
From the disobedience of the meek.
Checking for pursuers.
Struck by the silence, hoping God had changed His mind.
Our two daughters were already vanishing over the hilltop.
I felt age within me. Distance.
The futility of wandering. Torpor.
I looked back setting my bundle down.
I looked back not knowing where to set my foot.
Serpents appeared on my path,
spiders, field mice, baby vultures.
They were neither good nor evil now — every living thing
was simply creeping or hopping along in the mass panic.
I looked back in desolation.
In shame because we had stolen away.
Wanting to cry out, to go home.
Or only when a sudden gust of wind
unbound my hair and lifted up my robe.
It seemed to me that they were watching from the walls of Sodom
and bursting into thunderous laughter again and again.
I looked back in anger.
To savor their terrible fate.

I looked back for all the reasons given above.
I looked back involuntarily.
It was only a rock that turned underfoot, growling at me.
It was a sudden crack that stopped me in my tracks.
A hamster on its hind paws tottered on the edge.
It was then we both glanced back.
No, no. I ran on,
I crept, I flew upward
until darkness fell from the heavens
and with it scorching gravel and dead birds.
I couldn't breathe and spun around and around.
Anyone who saw me must have thought I was dancing.
It's not inconceivable that my eyes were open.
It's possible I fell facing the city.

Seen from Above

A dead beetle lies on the path through the field.
Three pairs of legs folded neatly on its belly.
Instead of death's confusion, tidiness and order.
The horror of this sight is moderate,
its scope is strictly local, from the wheat grass to the mint.
The grief is quarantined.
The sky is blue.

To preserve our peace of mind, animals die
more shallowly: they aren't deceased, they're dead.
They leave behind, we'd like to think, less feeling and less world,
departing, we suppose, from a stage less tragic.
Their meek souls never haunt us in the dark,
they know their place,
they show respect.

And so the dead beetle on the path
lies unmourned and shining in the sun.
One glance at it will do for meditation —
clearly nothing much has happened to it.
Important matters are reserved for us,
for our life and our death, a death
that always claims the right of way.

The Old Turtle's Dream

The old turtle dreams about a lettuce leaf,
when by that leaf, the Emperor appears.
A century hasn't changed him in the least.
To the turtle it's an ordinary affair.

The Emperor appears in part, at any rate.
The sun reflects on black shoes right below
two shapely calves in stockings, spotless white.
To the turtle this is just the status quo.

Two legs paused en route from Austerlitz to Jena,
above them, clouds where thunderous laughter roars.
You may doubt the scene in all its splendor,
and if that well-shod foot could be the Emperor's.

It's hard to recognize someone from snippets,
from the left foot only or the right.
The turtle doesn't know what he has witnessed.
His childhood memories are slight.

Emperor or not. How does it alter
the mystery of what the turtle sees?
The void has briefly yielded up a stranger
who flickers back to life! From heels to knees.

Experiment

As a short subject before the main feature—
in which the actors did their best
to make me cry and even laugh—
we were shown an interesting experiment
involving a head.

The head
a minute earlier was still attached to . . .
but now it was cut off.
Everyone could see that it didn't have a body.
The tubes dangling from the neck hooked it up to a machine
that kept its blood circulating.
The head
was doing just fine.

Without showing pain or even surprise,
it followed a moving flashlight with its eyes.
It pricked up its ears at the sound of a bell.
Its moist nose could tell
the smell of bacon from odorless oblivion,
and licking its chops with evident relish
it salivated its salute to physiology.

A dog's faithful head,
a dog's friendly head
squinted its eyes when stroked,
convinced that it was still part of a whole
that crooks its back if patted
and wags its tail.

I thought about happiness and was frightened.
For if that's all life is about,
the head
was happy.

Smiles

The world would rather *see* hope than just hear
its song. And that's why statesmen have to smile.
Their pearly whites mean they're still full of cheer.
The game's complex, the goal's far out of reach,
the outcome's still unclear – once in a while
we need a friendly, gleaming set of teeth.

Heads of state must display unfurrowed brows
on airport runways, in the conference room.
They must embody one big, toothy "Wow!"
while pressing flesh or pressing urgent issues.
Their faces' self-regenerating tissues
make our hearts hum and our lenses zoom.

Dentistry turned to diplomatic skill
promises us a Golden Age tomorrow.
The going's rough, and so we need the laugh
of bright incisors, molars of goodwill.
Our times are still not safe and sane enough
for faces to show ordinary sorrow.

Dreamers keep saying, "Human brotherhood
will make this place a smiling paradise."
I'm not convinced. The statesman, in that case,
would not require facial exercise,
except from time to time: he's feeling good,
he's glad it's spring, and so he moves his face.
But human beings are, by nature, sad.
So be it, then. It isn't all that bad.

Military Parade

Ground-to-ground,
ground-to-air-to-ground,
air-to-water-to-ground-to-ground-to-water,
water-to-air-to-ground-to-air-to-air,
ground-to-water-to-air-to-water-to-air-to-ground,
air-to-ground-to-ground-to-ground-to-ground,

Some Ground Air Water-

The Terrorist, He's Watching

The bomb in the bar will explode at thirteen twenty.
Now it's just thirteen sixteen.
There's still time for some to go in
and some to come out.

The terrorist has already crossed the street.
The distance keeps him out of danger,
and what a view — just like the movies:

A woman in a yellow jacket, she's going in.
A man in dark glasses, he's coming out.
Teenagers in jeans, they're talking.
Thirteen seventeen and four seconds.
The short one, he's lucky, he's getting on a scooter,
but the tall one, he's going in.

Thirteen seventeen and forty seconds.
That girl, she's walking along with a green ribbon in her hair.
But then a bus suddenly pulls in front of her.
Thirteen eighteen.
The girl's gone.
Was she that dumb, did she go in or not,
we'll see when they carry them out.

Thirteen nineteen.
Somehow no one's going in.
Another guy, fat, bald, is leaving, though.
Wait a second, looks like he's looking for something in his
pockets and
at thirteen twenty minus ten seconds
he goes back in for his crummy gloves.

Thirteen twenty exactly.
This waiting, it's taking forever.
Any second now.
No, not yet.
Yes, now.
The bomb, it explodes.

A Medieval Miniature

Up the verdantest of hills,
in this most equestrian of pageants,
wearing the silkiest of cloaks.

Toward a castle with seven towers,
each of them by far the tallest.

In the foreground, a duke,
most flatteringly unrotund;
by his side, his duchess,
young and fair beyond compare.

Behind them, the ladies-in-waiting,
all pretty as pictures, verily,
then a page, the most ladsome of lads,
and perched upon his pagey shoulder
something exceedingly monkeylike,
endowed with the drollest of faces
and tails.

Following close behind, three knights,
all chivalry and rivalry,
so if the first is fearsome of countenance,
the next one strives to be more daunting still,
and if he prances on a bay steed
the third will prance upon a bayer,
and all twelve hooves dance glancingly
atop the most wayside of daisies.

Whereas whosoever is downcast and weary,
cross-eyed and out at elbows,
is most manifestly left out of the scene.

Even the least pressing of questions,
burgherish or peasantish,
cannot survive beneath this most azure of skies.

And not even the eaglest of eyes
could spy even the tiniest of gallows —
nothing casts the slightest shadow of a doubt.

Thus they proceed most pleasantly
through this feudalest of realisms.

This same, however, has seen to the scene's balance:
it has given them their Hell in the next frame.
Oh yes, all that went without
even the silentest of sayings.

Aging Opera Singer

"Today he sings this way: tralala tra la.
But I sang it like this: tralala tra la.
Do you hear the difference?
And instead of standing here, he stands here
and looks this way, not this way,
although she comes flying in from over there,
not over there, and not like today rampa pampa pam,
but quite simply rampa pampa pam,
the unforgettable Tschubek-Bombonieri,
only
who remembers her now—"

In Praise of My Sister

My sister doesn't write poems,
and it's unlikely that she'll suddenly start writing poems.
She takes after her mother, who didn't write poems,
and also her father, who likewise didn't write poems.
I feel safe beneath my sister's roof:
my sister's husband would rather die than write poems.
And, even though this is starting to sound as repetitive as
    Peter Piper,
the truth is, none of my relatives write poems.

My sister's desk drawers don't hold old poems,
and her handbag doesn't hold new ones.
When my sister asks me over for lunch,
I know she doesn't want to read me her poems.
Her soups are delicious without ulterior motives.
Her coffee doesn't spill on manuscripts.

There are many families in which nobody writes poems,
but once it starts up it's hard to quarantine.
Sometimes poetry cascades down through the generations,
creating fatal whirlpools where family love may founder.

My sister has tackled oral prose with some success,
but her entire written opus consists of postcards from vacations
whose text is only the same promise every year:
when she gets back, she'll have
so much
much
much to tell.

Hermitage

You expected a hermit to live in the wilderness,
but he has a little house and a garden,
surrounded by cheerful birch groves,
ten minutes off the highway.
Just follow the signs.

You don't have to gaze at him through binoculars from afar.
You can see and hear him right up close,
while he's patiently explaining to a tour group from Wieliczka
why he's chosen strict isolation.

He wears a grayish habit,
and he has a long white beard,
cheeks pink as a baby's,
and bright blue eyes.
He'll gladly pose before the rosebush
for color photographs.

His picture is being taken by one Stanley Kowalik of Chicago,
who promises prints once they're developed.

Meanwhile a tight-lipped old lady from Bydgoszcz
whom no one visits but the meter reader
is writing in the guest book:
"God be praised
for letting me
see a genuine hermit before I die."

Teenagers write, too, using knives on trees:
"The Spirituals of '75 — meeting down below."

But what's Spot up to, where has Spot gone?
He's underneath the bench pretending he's a wolf.

Portrait of a Woman

She must be a variety.
Change so that nothing will change.
It's easy, impossible, tough going, worth a shot.
Her eyes are, as required, deep blue, gray,
dark, merry, full of pointless tears.
She sleeps with him as if she's first in line or the only one
    on earth.
She'll bear him four children, no children, one.
Naïve, but gives the best advice.
Weak, but takes on anything.
A screw loose and tough as nails.
Curls up with Jaspers or *Ladies' Home Journal.*
Can't figure out this bolt and builds a bridge.
Young, young as ever, still looking young.
Holds in her hands a baby sparrow with a broken wing,
her own money for some trip far away,
a meat cleaver, a compress, a glass of vodka.
Where's she running, isn't she exhausted.
Not a bit, a little, to death, it doesn't matter.
She must love him, or she's just plain stubborn.
For better, for worse, for heaven's sake.

Evaluation of an Unwritten Poem

In the poem's opening words
the authoress asserts that while the Earth is small,
the sky is excessively large and
in it there are, I quote, "too many stars for our own good."

In her depiction of the sky, one detects a certain helplessness,
the authoress is lost in a terrifying expanse,
she is startled by the planets' lifelessness,
and within her mind (which can only be called imprecise)
a question soon arises:
whether we are, in the end, alone
under the sun, all suns that ever shone.

In spite of all the laws of probability!
And today's universally accepted assumptions!
In the face of the irrefutable evidence that may fall
into human hands any day now! That's poetry for you.

Meanwhile, our Lady Bard returns to Earth,
a planet, so she claims, which "makes its rounds without
    eyewitnesses,"
the only "science fiction that our cosmos can afford."
The despair of a Pascal (1623–1662, *note mine*)
is, the authoress implies, unrivaled
on any, say, Andromeda or Cassiopeia.
Our solitary existence exacerbates our sense of obligation,
and raises the inevitable question, How are we to live et cetera?
since "we can't avoid the void."
"'My God,' man calls out to Himself,
'have mercy on me, I beseech thee, show me the way . . .'"

The authoress is distressed by the thought of life squandered
so freely,
as if our supplies were boundless.
She is likewise worried by wars, which are, in her perverse
opinion,
always lost on both sides,
and by the "authoritorture" (*sic!*) of some people by others.
Her moralistic intentions glimmer throughout the poem.
They might shine brighter beneath a less naïve pen.

Not under this one, alas. Her fundamentally unpersuasive thesis
(that we may well be, in the end, alone
under the sun, all suns that ever shone)
combined with her lackadaisical style (a mixture
of lofty rhetoric and ordinary speech)
forces the question: Whom might this piece convince?
The answer can only be: No one. *QED.*

Warning

Don't take jesters into outer space,
that's my advice.

Fourteen lifeless planets,
a few comets, two stars.
By the time you take off for the third star,
your jesters will be out of humor.

The cosmos is what it is—
namely, perfect.
Your jesters will never forgive it.

Nothing will make them happy:
not time (too immemorial),
not beauty (no flaws),
not gravity (no use for levity).
While others drop their jaws in awe,
the jesters will just yawn.

En route to the fourth star
things will only get worse.
Curdled smiles,
disrupted sleep and equilibrium,
idle chatter:
remember that crow with the cheese in its beak,
the fly droppings on His Majesty's portrait,
the monkey in the steaming bath—
now that was living.

Narrow-minded.
They'll take Thursday over infinity any day.
Primitive.
Out of tune suits them better than the music of the spheres.
They're happiest in the cracks
between theory and practice,
cause and effect.
But this is Space, not Earth: everything's a perfect fit.

On the thirtieth planet
(with an eye to its impeccable desolation)
they'll refuse even to leave their cubicles:
"My head aches," they'll complain. "I stubbed my toe."

What a waste. What a disgrace.
So much good money lost in outer space.

The Onion

The onion, now that's something else.
Its innards don't exist.
Nothing but pure onionhood
fills this devout onionist.
Oniony on the inside,
onionesque it appears.
It follows its own daimonion
without our human tears.

Our skin is just a cover-up
for the land where none dare go,
an internal inferno,
the anathema of anatomy.
In an onion there's only onion
from its top to its toe,
onionymous monomania,
unanimous omninudity.

At peace, of a piece,
internally at rest.
Inside it, there's a smaller one
of undiminished worth.
The second holds a third one,
the third contains a fourth.
A centripetal fugue.
Polyphony compressed.

Nature's rotundest tummy,
its greatest success story,
the onion drapes itself in its
own aureoles of glory.
We hold veins, nerves, and fat,
secretions' secret sections.
Not for us such idiotic
onionoid perfections.

The Suicide's Room

I'll bet you think the room was empty.
Wrong. There were three chairs with sturdy backs.
A lamp, good for fighting the dark.
A desk, and on the desk a wallet, some newspapers.
A carefree Buddha and a worried Christ.
Seven lucky elephants, a notebook in a drawer.
You think our addresses weren't in it?

No books, no pictures, no records, you guess?
Wrong. A comforting trumpet poised in black hands.
Saskia and her cordial little flower.
Joy the spark of gods.
Odysseus stretched on the shelf in life-giving sleep
after the labors of Book Five.
The moralists
with the golden syllables of their names
inscribed on finely tanned spines.
Next to them, the politicians braced their backs.

No way out? But what about the door?
No prospects? The window had other views.
His glasses
lay on the windowsill.
And one fly buzzed — that is, was still alive.

You think at least the note must tell us something.
But what if I say there was no note —
and he had so many friends, but all of us fit neatly
inside the empty envelope propped up against a cup.

Apple Tree

In heavenly May, under an apple tree, lovely
and bursting with blossoms like peals of laughter,

under something unruffled by both good and evil,
under something that rustles its branches regardless,

under no one's, no matter what anyone calls it,
under something that bears just a foretaste of fruit,

under something not caring which year and what country,
what kind of planet and where it is rolling,

under something so distant, so different from me,
that it neither heartens nor horrifies me,

under something untroubled by whatever happens,
under something whose every leaf trembles with patience,

under something as puzzling as if I had dreamed it,
or had dreamed not it but everything else,
all too completely and conceitedly —

to linger longer, not to go home again.
Since only prisoners want to go home.

In Praise of Feeling Bad about Yourself

The buzzard never says it is to blame.
The panther wouldn't know what scruples mean.
When the piranha strikes, it feels no shame.
If snakes had hands, they'd claim their hands were clean.

A jackal doesn't understand remorse.
Lions and lice don't waver in their course.
Why should they, when they know they're right?

Though hearts of killer whales may weigh a ton,
in every other way they're light.

On this third planet of the sun
among the signs of bestiality
a clear conscience is number one.

Life While-You-Wait

Life While-You-Wait.
Performance without rehearsal.
Body without alterations.
Head without premeditation.

I know nothing of the role I play.
I only know it's mine, I can't exchange it.

I have to guess on the spot
just what this play's all about.

Ill-prepared for the privilege of living,
I can barely keep up with the pace that the action demands.
I improvise, although I loathe improvisation.
I trip at every step over my own ignorance.
I can't conceal my hayseed manners.
My instincts are for hammy histrionics.
Stage fright makes excuses for me, which humiliate me more.
Extenuating circumstances strike me as cruel.

Words and impulses you can't take back,
stars you'll never get counted,
your character like a raincoat you button on the run —
the pitiful results of all this unexpectedness.

If I could just rehearse one Wednesday in advance,
or repeat a single Thursday that has passed!
But here comes Friday with a script I haven't seen.
Is it fair, I ask
(my voice a little hoarse,
since I couldn't even clear my throat offstage).

You'd be wrong to think that it's just a slapdash quiz
taken in makeshift accommodations. Oh no.
I'm standing on the set and I see how strong it is.
The props are surprisingly precise.
The machine rotating the stage has been around even longer.
The farthest galaxies have been turned on.
Oh no, there's no question, this must be the premiere.
And whatever I do
will become forever what I've done.

On the Banks of the Styx

Dear individual soul, this is the Styx.
The Styx, that's right. Why are you so perplexed?
As soon as Charon reads the prepared text
over the speakers, let the nymphs affix
your name badge and transport you to the banks.
(The nymphs? They fled your woods and joined the ranks
of personnel here.) Floodlights will reveal
piers built of reinforced concrete and steel,
and hovercrafts whose beelike buzz resounds
where Charon used to ply his wooden oar.
Mankind has multiplied, has burst its bounds:
nothing, sweet soul, is as it was before.
Skyscrapers, solid waste, and dirty air:
the scenery's been harmed beyond repair.
Safe and efficient transportation (millions
of souls served here, all races, creeds, and sexes)
requires urban planning: hence pavilions,
warehouses, dry docks, and office complexes.
Among the gods it's Hermes, my dear soul,
who makes all prophecies and estimations
when revolutions and wars take their toll—
our boats, of course, require reservations.
A one-way trip across the Styx is free:
the meters saying "No Canadian dimes,
no tokens" are left standing, as you see,
but only to remind us of old times.
From Section Tau Four of the Alpha Pier
you're boarding hovercraft Sigma Sixteen—
it's packed with sweating souls, but in the rear

you'll find a seat (I've got it on my screen).
Now Tartarus (let me pull up the file)
is overbooked, too — no way we could stretch it.
Cramped, crumpled souls all dying to get out,
one last half drop of Lethe in my phial . . .
Not faith in the beyond, but only doubt
can make you, sorry soul, a bit less wretched.

Utopia

Island where all becomes clear.

Solid ground beneath your feet.

The only roads are those that offer access.

Bushes bend beneath the weight of proofs.

The Tree of Valid Supposition grows here
with branches disentangled since time immemorial.

The Tree of Understanding, dazzlingly straight and simple,
sprouts by the spring called Now I Get It.

The thicker the woods, the vaster the vista:
the Valley of Obviously.

If any doubts arise, the wind dispels them instantly.

Echoes stir unsummoned
and eagerly explain all the secrets of the worlds.

On the right a cave where Meaning lies.

On the left the Lake of Deep Conviction.
Truth breaks from the bottom and bobs to the surface.

Unshakable Confidence towers over the valley.
Its peak offers an excellent view of the Essence of Things.

For all its charms, the island is uninhabited,
and the faint footprints scattered on its beaches
turn without exception to the sea.

As if all you can do here is leave
and plunge, never to return, into the depths.

Into unfathomable life.

Pi

The admirable number pi:
three point one four one
All the following digits are also initial,
five nine two because it never ends.
It can't be comprehended *six five three five* at a glance,
eight nine by calculation,
seven nine or imagination,
not even *three two three eight* by wit, that is, by comparison
four six to anything else
two six four three in the world.
The longest snake on earth calls it quits at about forty feet.
Likewise, snakes of myth and legend, though they may hold out a
    bit longer.
The pageant of digits comprising the number pi
doesn't stop at the page's edge.
It goes on across the table, through the air,
over a wall, a leaf, a bird's nest, clouds, straight into the sky,
through all the bottomless, bloated heavens.
Oh how brief—a mouse tail, a pigtail—is the tail of a comet!
How feeble the star's ray, bent by bumping up against space!
While here we have *two three fifteen three hundred nineteen*
my phone number your shirt size the year
nineteen hundred and seventy-three the sixth floor
the number of inhabitants sixty-five cents
hip measurement two fingers a charade, a code,
in which we find *hail to thee, blithe spirit, bird thou never wert*
alongside *ladies and gentlemen, no cause for alarm,*
as well as *heaven and earth shall pass away,*
but not the number pi, oh no, nothing doing,

it keeps right on with its rather remarkable *five,*
its uncommonly fine *eight,*
its far from final *seven,*
nudging, always nudging a sluggish eternity
to continue.

THE PEOPLE ON THE BRIDGE

1986

Stage Fright

Poets and writers.
So the saying goes.
That is poets aren't writers, but who—

Poets are poetry, writers are prose—

Prose can hold anything including poetry,
but in poetry there's only room for poetry—

In keeping with the poster that announces it
with a fin-de-siècle flourish of its giant P
framed in a winged lyre's strings
I shouldn't simply walk in, I should fly—

And wouldn't I be better off barefoot
to escape the clump and squeak
of cut-rate sneakers,
a clumsy ersatz angel—

If at least the dress were longer and more flowing
and the poems appeared not from a handbag but by sleight
of hand,
dressed in their Sunday best from head to toe,
with bells on, ding to dong,
ab ab ba—

On the platform lurks a little table
suggesting séances, with gilded legs,
and on the little table smokes a little candlestick—

Which means
I've got to read by candlelight
what I wrote by the light of an ordinary bulb
to the typewriter's tap tap tap —

Without worrying in advance
if it was poetry
and if so, what kind —

The kind in which prose is inappropriate
or the kind which is apropos in prose —

And what's the difference,
seen now only in half-light
against a crimson curtain's
purple fringe?

Surplus

A new star has been discovered,
which doesn't mean that things have gotten brighter
or that something we've been missing has appeared.

The star is large and distant,
so distant that it's small,
even smaller than others
much smaller than it.
Small wonder, then, if we were struck with wonder;
as we would be if only we had the time.

The star's age, mass, location —
all this perhaps will do
for one doctoral dissertation
and a wine-and-cheese reception
in circles close to the sky:
the astronomer, his wife, friends, and relations,
casual, congenial, come as you are,
mostly chat on earthbound topics,
surrounded by cozy earthtones.

The star's superb,
but that's no reason
why we can't drink to the ladies
who are incalculably closer.

The star's inconsequential.
It has no impact on the weather, fashion, final score,
government shakeups, moral crises, take-home pay.

No effect on propaganda or on heavy industry.
It's not reflected in a conference table's shine.
It's supernumerary in the light of life's numbered days.

What's the use of asking
under how many stars man is born
and under how many in a moment he will die.

A new one.
"At least show me where it is."
"Between that gray cloud's jagged edge
and the acacia twig over there on the left."
"I see," I say.

Archeology

Well, my poor man,
seems we've made some progress in my field.
Millennia have passed
since you first called me archeology.

I no longer require
your stone gods,
your ruins with legible inscriptions.

Show me your whatever
and I'll tell you who you were.
Something's bottom,
something's top.
A scrap of engine. A picture tube's neck.
An inch of cable. Fingers turned to dust.
Or even less than that, or even less.

Using a method
that you couldn't have known then,
I can stir up memory
in countless elements.
Traces of blood are forever.
Lies shine.
Secret codes resound.
Doubts and intentions come to light.

If I want to
(and you can't be too sure
that I will),
I'll peer down the throat of your silence,
I'll read your views

from the sockets of your eyes,
I'll remind you in infinite detail
of what you expected from life besides death.

Show me your nothing
that you've left behind
and I'll build from it a forest and a highway,
an airport, baseness, tenderness,
a missing home.

Show me your little poem
and I'll tell you why it wasn't written
any earlier or later than it was.

Oh no, you've got me wrong.
Keep your funny piece of paper
with its scribbles.
All I need for my ends
is your layer of dirt
and the long-gone
smell of burning.

View with a Grain of Sand

We call it a grain of sand,
but it calls itself neither grain nor sand.
It does just fine without a name,
whether general, particular,
permanent, passing,
incorrect, or apt.

Our glance, our touch mean nothing to it.
It doesn't feel itself seen and touched.
And that it fell on the windowsill
is only our experience, not its.
For it, it is no different from falling on anything else
with no assurance that it has finished falling
or that it is falling still.

The window has a wonderful view of a lake,
but the view doesn't view itself.
It exists in this world
colorless, shapeless,
soundless, odorless, and painless.

The lake's floor exists floorlessly,
and its shore exists shorelessly.
Its water feels itself neither wet nor dry
and its waves to themselves are neither singular nor plural.
They splash deaf to their own noise
on pebbles neither large nor small.

And all this beneath a sky by nature skyless
in which the sun sets without setting at all
and hides without hiding behind an unminding cloud.

The wind ruffles it, its only reason being
that it blows.

A second passes.
A second second.
A third.
But they're three seconds only for us.

Time has passed like a courier with urgent news.
But that's just our simile.
The character is invented, his haste is make-believe,
his news inhuman.

Clothes

You take off, we take off, they take off
coats, jackets, blouses, double-breasted suits,
made of wool, cotton, cotton-polyester,
skirts, shirts, underwear, slacks, slips, socks,
putting, hanging, tossing them across
the backs of chairs, the wings of metal screens;
for now, the doctor says, it's not too bad,
you may get dressed, get rested up, get out of town,
take one in case, at bedtime, after lunch,
show up in a couple of months, next spring, next year;
you see, and you thought, and we were afraid that,
and he imagined, and you all believed;
it's time to tie, to fasten with shaking hands
shoelaces, buckles, velcro, zippers, snaps,
belts, buttons, cuff links, collars, neckties, clasps
and to pull out of handbags, pockets, sleeves
a crumpled, dotted, flowered, checkered scarf
whose usefulness has suddenly been prolonged.

On Death, Without Exaggeration

It can't take a joke,
find a star, make a bridge.
It knows nothing about weaving, mining, farming,
building ships, or baking cakes.

In our planning for tomorrow,
it has the final word,
which is always beside the point.

It can't even get the things done
that are part of its trade:
dig a grave,
make a coffin,
clean up after itself.

Preoccupied with killing,
it does the job awkwardly,
without system or skill.
As though each of us were its first kill.

Oh, it has its triumphs,
but look at its countless defeats,
missed blows,
and repeat attempts!

Sometimes it isn't strong enough
to swat a fly from the air.
Many are the caterpillars
that have outcrawled it.

All those bulbs, pods,
tentacles, fins, tracheae,
nuptial plumage, and winter fur
show that it has fallen behind
with its halfhearted work.

Ill will won't help
and even our lending a hand with wars and coups d'état
is so far not enough.

Hearts beat inside eggs.
Babies' skeletons grow.
Seeds, hard at work, sprout their first tiny pair of leaves
and sometimes even tall trees far away.

Whoever claims that it's omnipotent
is himself living proof
that it's not.

There's no life
that couldn't be immortal
if only for a moment.

Death
always arrives by that very moment too late.

In vain it tugs at the knob
of the invisible door.
As far as you've come
can't be undone.

The Great Man's House

The marble tells us in golden syllables:
Here the great man lived, and worked, and died.
Here are the garden paths where he personally scattered
    the gravel.
Here's the bench — don't touch — he hewed the stone himself.
And here — watch the steps — we enter the house.

He managed to come into the world at what was still a
    fitting time.
All that was to pass passed in this house.
Not in housing projects,
not in furnished but empty quarters,
among unknown neighbors,
on fifteenth floors
that student field trips rarely reach.

In this room he thought,
in this alcove he slept,
and here he entertained his guests.
Portraits, armchair, desk, pipe, globe,
flute, well-worn carpet, glassed-in porch.
Here he exchanged bows with the tailor and shoemaker
who made his coats and boots to order.

It's not the same as photographs in boxes,
dried-out ballpoint pens in plastic cups,
store-bought clothes in store-bought closets,
a window that looks out on clouds, not passersby.

Was he happy? Sad?
That's not the point.
He still made confessions in letters
without thinking they'd be opened en route.
He still kept a careful, candid diary
knowing it wouldn't be seized in a search.
The thing that most frightened him was a comet's flight.
The world's doom lay then in God's hands alone.

He was lucky enough to die not in a hospital,
not behind some white, anonymous screen.
There was still someone there at his bedside to memorize
his mumbled words.

As if he had been given
a reusable life:
he sent out books to be bound,
he didn't strike the names of the dead from his ledgers.
And the trees that he planted in the garden by his house
still grew for him as *juglans regia,*
and *quercus rubra,* and *ulmus,* and *larix,*
and *fraxinus excelsior.*

In Broad Daylight

He would
vacation in a mountain boardinghouse, he would
come down for lunch, from his
table by the window he would
scan the four spruces, branch to branch,
without shaking off the freshly fallen snow.

Goateed, balding,
gray-haired, in glasses,
with coarsened, weary features,
with a wart on his cheek and a furrowed forehead,
as if clay had covered up the angelic marble—he wouldn't
know himself when it all happened.
The price, after all, for not having died already
goes up not in leaps but step by step, and he would
pay that price, too.
About his ear, just grazed by the bullet
when he ducked at the last minute, he would
say: "I was damned lucky."

While waiting to be served his noodle soup, he would
read a paper with the current date,
giant headlines, the tiny print of ads,
or drum his fingers on the white tablecloth, and his hands would
have been used a long time now,
with their chapped skin and swollen veins.

Sometimes someone would
yell from the doorway: "Mr. Baczyński,* phone call for you" —
and there'd be nothing strange about that
being him, about him standing up, straightening his sweater,
and slowly moving toward the door.

At this sight no one would
stop talking, no one would
freeze in midgesture, midbreath,
because this commonplace event would
be treated — such a pity —
as a commonplace event.

* Krzysztof Kamil Baczyński, an enormously gifted poet of the "war generation," was killed as a Home Army fighter in the Warsaw Uprising of 1944 at the age of twenty-three. (*Translators' note*)

Our Ancestors' Short Lives

Few of them made it to thirty.
Old age was the privilege of rocks and trees.
Childhood ended as fast as wolf cubs grow.
One had to hurry, to get on with life
before the sun went down,
before the first snow.

Thirteen-year-olds bearing children,
four-year-olds stalking birds' nests in the rushes,
leading the hunt at twenty—
they aren't yet, then they are gone.
Infinity's ends fused quickly.
Witches chewed charms
with all the teeth of youth intact.
A son grew to manhood beneath his father's eye.
Beneath the grandfather's blank sockets the grandson was born.

And anyway they didn't count the years.
They counted nets, pods, sheds, and axes.
Time, so generous toward any petty star in the sky,
offered them a nearly empty hand
and quickly took it back, as if the effort were too much.
One step more, two steps more
along the glittering river
that sprang from darkness and vanished into darkness.

There wasn't a moment to lose,
no deferred questions, no belated revelations,
just those experienced in time.
Wisdom couldn't wait for gray hair.
It had to see clearly before it saw the light
and to hear every voice before it sounded.

Good and evil —
they knew little of them, but knew all:
when evil triumphs, good goes into hiding;
when good is manifest, then evil lies low.
Neither can be conquered
or cast off beyond return.
Hence, if joy, then with a touch of fear;
if despair, then not without some quiet hope.
Life, however long, will always be short.
Too short for anything to be added.

Hitler's First Photograph

And who's this little fellow in his itty-bitty robe?
That's tiny baby Adolf, the Hitlers' little boy!
Will he grow up to be an LLD?
Or a tenor in Vienna's Opera House?
Whose teensy hand is this, whose little ear and eye and nose?
Whose tummy full of milk, we just don't know:
printer's, doctor's, merchant's, priest's?
Where will those tootsy-wootsies finally wander?
To a garden, to a school, to an office, to a bride?
Maybe to the Bürgermeister's daughter?

Precious little angel, mommy's sunshine, honey bun.
While he was being born, a year ago,
there was no dearth of signs on the earth and in the sky:
spring sun, geraniums in windows,
the organ grinder's music in the yard,
a lucky fortune wrapped in rosy paper.
Then just before the labor his mother's fateful dream.
A dove seen in a dream means joyful news —
if it is caught, a long-awaited guest will come.
Knock knock, who's there, it's Adolf's heartchen knocking.

A little pacifier, diaper, rattle, bib,
our bouncing boy, thank God and knock on wood, is well,
looks just like his folks, like a kitten in a basket,
like the tots in every other family album.
Sh-h-h, let's not start crying, sugar.
The camera will click from under that black hood.

The Klinger Atelier, Grabenstrasse, Braunau.
And Braunau is a small but worthy town—
honest businesses, obliging neighbors,
smell of yeast dough, of gray soap.
No one hears howling dogs, or fate's footsteps.
A history teacher loosens his collar
and yawns over homework.

The Century's Decline

Our twentieth century was going to improve on the others.
It will never prove it now,
now that its years are numbered,
its gait is shaky,
its breath is short.

Too many things have happened
that weren't supposed to happen,
and what was supposed to come about
has not.

Happiness and spring, among other things,
were supposed to be getting closer.

Fear was expected to leave the mountains and the valleys.
Truth was supposed to hit home
before a lie.

A couple of problems weren't going
to come up anymore:
hunger, for example,
and war, and so forth.

There was going to be respect
for helpless people's helplessness,
trust, that kind of stuff.

Anyone who planned to enjoy the world
is now faced
with a hopeless task.

Stupidity isn't funny.
Wisdom isn't gay.
Hope
isn't that young girl anymore,
et cetera, alas.

God was finally going to believe
in a man both good and strong,
but good and strong
are still two different men.

"How should we live?" someone asked me in a letter.
I had meant to ask him
the same question.

Again, and as ever,
as may be seen above,
the most pressing questions
are naïve ones.

Children of Our Age

We are children of our age,
it's a political age.

All day long, all through the night,
all affairs — yours, ours, theirs —
are political affairs.

Whether you like it or not,
your genes have a political past,
your skin, a political cast,
your eyes, a political slant.

Whatever you say reverberates,
whatever you don't say speaks for itself.
So either way you're talking politics.

Even when you take to the woods,
you're taking political steps
on political grounds.

Apolitical poems are also political,
and above us shines a moon
no longer purely lunar.
To be or not to be, that is the question.
And though it troubles the digestion
it's a question, as always, of politics.

To acquire a political meaning
you don't even have to be human.
Raw material will do,
or protein feed, or crude oil,

or a conference table whose shape
was quarreled over for months:
Should we arbitrate life and death
at a round table or a square one?

Meanwhile, people perished,
animals died,
houses burned,
and the fields ran wild
just as in times immemorial
and less political.

Tortures

Nothing has changed.
The body is a reservoir of pain;
it has to eat and breathe the air, and sleep;
it has thin skin and the blood is just beneath it;
it has a good supply of teeth and fingernails;
its bones can be broken; its joints can be stretched.
In tortures, all of this is considered.

Nothing has changed.
The body still trembles as it trembled
before Rome was founded and after,
in the twentieth century before and after Christ.
Tortures are just what they were, only the earth has shrunk
and whatever goes on sounds as if it's just a room away.

Nothing has changed.
Except there are more people,
and new offenses have sprung up beside the old ones —
real, make-believe, short-lived, and nonexistent.
But the cry with which the body answers for them
was, is, and will be a cry of innocence
in keeping with the age-old scale and pitch.

Nothing has changed.
Except perhaps the manners, ceremonies, dances.
The gesture of the hands shielding the head
has nonetheless remained the same.
The body writhes, jerks, and tugs,
falls to the ground when shoved, pulls up its knees,
bruises, swells, drools, and bleeds.

Nothing has changed.
Except the run of rivers,
the shapes of forests, shores, deserts, and glaciers.
The little soul roams among those landscapes,
disappears, returns, draws near, moves away,
evasive and a stranger to itself,
now sure, now uncertain of its own existence,
whereas the body is and is and is
and has nowhere to go.

Plotting with the Dead

Under what conditions do you dream of the dead?
Do you often think of them before you fall asleep?
Who appears first?
Is it always the same one?
First name? Surname? Cemetery? Date deceased?

To what do they refer?
Old friendship? Kinship? Fatherland?
Do they say where they come from?
And who's behind them?
And who besides you sees them in his dreams?

Their faces, are they like their photographs?
Have they aged at all with time?
Are they robust? Are they wan?
The murdered ones, have their wounds healed yet?
Do they still remember who killed them?

What do they hold in their hands? Describe these objects.
Are they charred? Moldy? Rusty? Decomposed?
And in their eyes, what? Entreaty? A threat? Be specific.
Do you only chat about the weather?
Or about flowers? Birds? Butterflies?

No awkward questions on their part?
If so, what do you reply?
Instead of safely keeping quiet?
Or evasively changing the dream's subject?
Or waking up just in time?

Writing a Résumé

What needs to be done?
Fill out the application
and enclose the résumé.

Regardless of the length of life,
a résumé is best kept short.

Concise, well-chosen facts are de rigueur.
Landscapes are replaced by addresses,
shaky memories give way to unshakable dates.

Of all your loves, mention only the marriage;
of all your children, only those who were born.

Who knows you matters more than whom you know.
Trips only if taken abroad.
Memberships in what but without why.
Honors, but not how they were earned.

Write as if you'd never talked to yourself
and always kept yourself at arm's length.

Pass over in silence your dogs, cats, birds,
dusty keepsakes, friends, and dreams.

Price, not worth,
and title, not what's inside.
His shoe size, not where he's off to,
that one you pass off as yourself.
In addition, a photograph with one ear showing.
What matters is its shape, not what it hears.
What is there to hear, anyway?
The clatter of paper shredders.

Funeral (II)

“so suddenly, who could have seen it coming”
“stress and smoking, I kept telling him”
“not bad, thanks, and you”
“these flowers need to be unwrapped”
“his brother’s heart gave out, too, it runs in the family”
“I’d never know you in that beard”
“he was asking for it, always mixed up in something”
“that new guy was going to make a speech, I don’t see him”
“Kazek’s in Warsaw, Tadek has gone abroad”
“you were smart, you brought the only umbrella”
“so what if he was more talented than they were”
“no, it’s a walk-through room, Barbara won’t take it”
“of course, he was right, but that’s no excuse”
“with body work and paint, just guess how much”
“two egg yolks and a tablespoon of sugar”
“none of his business, what was in it for him”
“only in blue and just small sizes”
“five times and never any answer”
“all right, so I could have, but you could have, too”
“good thing that at least she still had a job”
“don’t know, relatives, I guess”
“that priest looks just like Belmondo”
“I’ve never been in this part of the grounds”
“I dreamed about him last week, I had a feeling”
“his daughter’s not bad-looking”
“the way of all flesh”
“give my best to the widow, I’ve got to run”
“it all sounded so much more solemn in Latin”
“what’s gone is gone”

"goodbye"
"I could sure use a drink"
"give me a call"
"which bus goes downtown"
"I'm going this way"
"we're not"

An Opinion on the Question of Pornography

There's nothing more debauched than thinking.
This sort of wantonness runs wild like a wind-borne weed
on a plot laid out for daisies.

Nothing's sacred for those who think.
Calling things brazenly by name,
risqué analyses, salacious syntheses,
frenzied, rakish chases after the bare facts,
the filthy fingering of touchy subjects,
discussion in heat — it's music to their ears.

In broad daylight or under cover of night
they form circles, triangles, or pairs.
The partners' age and sex are unimportant.
Their eyes glitter, their cheeks are flushed.
Friend leads friend astray.
Degenerate daughters corrupt their fathers.
A brother pimps for his little sister.

They prefer the fruits
from the forbidden tree of knowledge
to the pink buttocks found in glossy magazines —
all that ultimately simple-hearted smut.
The books they relish have no pictures.
What variety they have lies in certain phrases
marked with a thumbnail or a crayon.

It's shocking, the positions,
the unchecked simplicity with which
one mind contrives to fertilize another!
Such positions the Kama Sutra itself doesn't know.

During these trysts of theirs, the only thing that's steamy
    is the tea.
People sit on their chairs and move their lips.
Everyone crosses only his own legs
so that one foot is resting on the floor
while the other dangles freely in midair.
Only now and then does somebody get up,
go to the window,
and through a crack in the curtains
take a peep out at the street.

A Tale Begun

The world is never ready
for the birth of a child.

Our ships are not yet back from Winnland.
We still have to get over the S. Gothard pass.
We've got to outwit the watchmen on the desert of Thor,
fight our way through the sewers to Warsaw's center,
gain access to King Harald the Butterpat,
and wait until the downfall of Minister Fouché.
Only in Acapulco
can we begin anew.

We've run out of bandages,
matches, hydraulic presses, arguments, and water.
We haven't got the trucks, we haven't got the Minghs' support.
This skinny horse won't be enough to bribe the sheriff.
No news so far about the Tartars' captives.
We'll need a warmer cave for winter
and someone who can speak Harari.

We don't know whom to trust in Nineveh,
what conditions the Prince-Cardinal will decree,
which names Beria has still got inside his files.
They say Karol the Hammer strikes tomorrow at dawn.
In this situation, let's appease Cheops,
report ourselves of our own free will,
change faiths,
pretend to be friends with the Doge,
and say that we've got nothing to do with the Kwabe tribe.

Time to light the fires.
Let's send a cable to grandma in Zabierzów.
Let's untie the knots in the yurt's leather straps.

May delivery be easy,
may our child grow and be well.
Let him be happy from time to time
and leap over abysses.
Let his heart have strength to endure
and his mind be awake and reach far.

But not so far
that it sees into the future.
Spare him
that one gift,
O heavenly powers.

Into the Ark

An endless rain is just beginning.
Into the ark, for where else can you go,
you poems for a single voice,
private exultations,
unnecessary talents,
surplus curiosity,
short-range sorrows and fears,
eagerness to see things from all six sides.

Rivers are swelling and bursting their banks.
Into the ark, all you chiaroscuros and half-tones,
you details, ornaments, and whims,
silly exceptions,
forgotten signs,
countless shades of the color gray,
play for play's sake,
and tears of mirth.

As far as the eye can see, there's water and hazy horizon.
Into the ark, plans for the distant future,
joy in difference,
admiration for the better man,
choice not narrowed down to one of two,
outworn scruples,
time to think it over,
and the belief that all this
will still come in handy someday.

For the sake of the children
that we still are,
fairy tales have happy endings.
That's the only finale that will do here, too.
The rain will stop,
the waves will subside,
the clouds will part
in the cleared-up sky,
and they'll be once more
what clouds overhead ought to be:
lofty and rather lighthearted
in their likeness to things
drying in the sun —
isles of bliss,
lambs,
cauliflowers,
diapers.

Possibilities

I prefer movies.
I prefer cats.
I prefer the oaks along the Warta.
I prefer Dickens to Dostoyevsky.
I prefer myself liking people
to myself loving mankind.
I prefer keeping a needle and thread on hand, just in case.
I prefer the color green.
I prefer not to maintain
that reason is to blame for everything.
I prefer exceptions.
I prefer to leave early.
I prefer talking to doctors about something else.
I prefer the old fine-lined illustrations.
I prefer the absurdity of writing poems
to the absurdity of not writing poems.
I prefer, where love's concerned, nonspecific anniversaries
that can be celebrated every day.
I prefer moralists
who promise me nothing.
I prefer cunning kindness to the overtrustful kind.
I prefer the earth in civvies.
I prefer conquered to conquering countries.
I prefer having some reservations.
I prefer the hell of chaos to the hell of order.
I prefer the Grimms' fairy tales to the newspapers' front pages.
I prefer leaves without flowers to flowers without leaves.
I prefer dogs with uncropped tails.
I prefer light eyes, since mine are dark.

I prefer desk drawers.
I prefer many things that I haven't mentioned here
to many things I've also left unsaid.
I prefer zeros on the loose
to those lined up behind a cipher.
I prefer the time of insects to the time of stars.
I prefer to knock on wood.
I prefer not to ask how much longer and when.
I prefer keeping in mind even the possibility
that existence has its own reason for being.

Miracle Fair

The commonplace miracle:
that so many common miracles take place.

The usual miracle:
invisible dogs barking
in the dead of night.

One of many miracles:
a small and airy cloud
is able to upstage the massive moon.

Several miracles in one:
an alder is reflected in the water
and is reversed from left to right
and grows from crown to root
and never hits bottom
though the water isn't deep.

A run-of-the-mill miracle:
winds mild to moderate
turning gusty in storms.

A miracle in the first place:
cows will be cows.

Next but not least:
just this cherry orchard
from just this cherry pit.

A miracle minus top hat and tails:
fluttering white doves.

A miracle (what else can you call it):
the sun rose today at three fourteen A.M.
and will set tonight at one past eight.

A miracle that's lost on us:
the hand actually has fewer than six fingers
but still it's got more than four.

A miracle, just take a look around:
the inescapable earth.

An extra miracle, extra and ordinary:
the unthinkable
can be thought.

The People on the Bridge

An odd planet, and those on it are odd, too.
They're subject to time, but they won't admit it.
They have their own ways of expressing protest.
They make up little pictures, like for instance this:

At first glance, nothing special.
What you see is water.
And one of its banks.
And a little boat sailing strenuously upstream.
And a bridge over the water, and people on the bridge.
It appears that the people are picking up their pace
because of the rain just beginning to lash down
from a dark cloud.

The thing is, nothing else happens.
The cloud doesn't change its color or its shape.
The rain doesn't increase or subside.
The boat sails on without moving.
The people on the bridge are running now
exactly where they ran before.

It's difficult at this point to keep from commenting.
This picture is by no means innocent.
Time has been stopped here.
Its laws are no longer consulted.
It has been relieved of its influence over the course of events.
It has been ignored and insulted.

On account of a rebel,
one Hiroshige Utagawa
(a being who, by the way,
died long ago and in due course),
time has tripped and fallen down.

It might well be simply a trifling prank,
an antic on the scale of just a couple of galaxies,
let us, however, just in case,
add one final comment for the record:

For generations, it's been considered good form here
to think highly of this picture,
to be entranced and moved.

There are those for whom even this is not enough.
They go so far as to hear the rain's spatter,
to feel the cold drops on their necks and backs,
they look at the bridge and the people on it
as if they saw themselves there,
running the same never-to-be-finished race
through the same endless, ever-to-be-covered distance,
and they have the nerve to believe
that this is really so.

THE END AND THE BEGINNING

1993

Sky

I should have begun with this: the sky.
A window minus sill, frame, and panes.
An aperture, nothing more,
but wide open.

I don't have to wait for a starry night,
I don't have to crane my neck
to get a look at it.
I've got the sky behind my back, at hand, and on my eyelids.
The sky binds me tight
and sweeps me off my feet.

Even the highest mountains
are no closer to the sky
than the deepest valleys.
There's no more of it in one place
than another.
A mole is no less in seventh heaven
than the owl spreading her wings.
The object that falls in an abyss
falls from sky to sky.

Grainy, gritty, liquid,
inflamed, or volatile
patches of sky, specks of sky,
gusts and heaps of sky.
The sky is everywhere,
even in the dark beneath your skin.
I eat the sky, I excrete the sky.

I'm a trap within a trap,
an inhabited inhabitant,
an embrace embraced,
a question answering a question.

Division into sky and earth—
it's not the proper way
to contemplate this wholeness.
It simply lets me go on living
at a more exact address
where I can be reached promptly
if I'm sought.
My identifying features
are rapture and despair.

No Title Required

It has come to this: I'm sitting under a tree
beside a river
on a sunny morning.
It's an insignificant event
and won't go down in history.
It's not battles and pacts,
where motives are scrutinized,
or noteworthy tyrannicides.

And yet I'm sitting by this river, that's a fact.
And since I'm here
I must have come from somewhere,
and before that
I must have turned up in many other places,
exactly like the conquerors of nations
before setting sail.

Even a passing moment has its fertile past,
its Friday before Saturday,
its May before June.
Its horizons are no less real
than those that a marshal's field glasses might scan.

This tree is a poplar that's been rooted here for years.
The river is the Raba; it didn't spring up yesterday.
The path leading through the bushes
wasn't beaten last week.
The wind had to blow the clouds here
before it could blow them away.

And though nothing much is going on nearby,
the world is no poorer in details for that.
It's just as grounded, just as definite
as when migrating races held it captive.

Conspiracies aren't the only things shrouded in silence.
Retinues of reasons don't trail coronations alone.
Anniversaries of revolutions may roll around,
but so do oval pebbles encircling the bay.

The tapestry of circumstance is intricate and dense.
Ants stitching in the grass.
The grass sewn into the ground.
The pattern of a wave being needled by a twig.

So it happens that I am and look.
Above me a white butterfly is fluttering through the air
on wings that are its alone,
and a shadow skims through my hands
that is none other than itself, no one else's but its own.

When I see such things, I'm no longer sure
that what's important
is more important than what's not.

Some People Like Poetry

Some people —
that means not everyone.
Not even most of them, only a few.
Not counting school, where you have to,
and poets themselves,
you might end up with something like two per thousand.

Like —
but then, you can like chicken noodle soup,
or compliments, or the color blue,
your old scarf,
your own way,
petting the dog.

Poetry —
but what is poetry anyway?
More than one rickety answer
has tumbled since that question first was raised.
But I just keep on not knowing, and I cling to that
like a redemptive handrail.

The End and the Beginning

After every war
someone has to tidy up.
Things won't pick
themselves up, after all.

Someone has to shove
the rubble to the roadsides
so the carts loaded with corpses
can get by.

Someone has to trudge
through sludge and ashes,
through the sofa springs,
the shards of glass,
the bloody rags.

Someone has to lug the post
to prop the wall,
someone has to glaze the window,
set the door in its frame.

No sound bites, no photo opportunities,
and it takes years.
All the cameras have gone
to other wars.

The bridges need to be rebuilt,
the railroad stations, too.
Shirtsleeves will be rolled
to shreds.

Someone, broom in hand,
still remembers how it was.
Someone else listens, nodding
his unshattered head.
But others are bound to be bustling nearby
who'll find all that
a little boring.

From time to time someone still must
dig up a rusted argument
from underneath a bush
and haul it off to the dump.

Those who knew
what this was all about
must make way for those
who know little.
And less than that.
And at last nothing less than nothing.

Someone has to lie there
in the grass that covers up
the causes and effects
with a cornstalk in his teeth,
gawking at clouds.

Hatred

See how efficient it still is,
how it keeps itself in shape—
our century's hatred.
How easily it vaults the tallest obstacles.
How rapidly it pounces, tracks us down.

It's not like other feelings.
At once both older and younger.
It gives birth itself to the reasons
that give it life.
When it sleeps, it's never eternal rest.
And sleeplessness won't sap its strength; it feeds it.

One religion or another—
whatever gets it ready, in position.
One fatherland or another—
whatever helps it get a running start.
Justice also works well at the outset
until hate gets its own momentum going.
Hatred. Hatred.
Its face twisted in a grimace
of erotic ecstasy.

Oh these other feelings,
listless weaklings.
Since when does brotherhood
draw crowds?
Has compassion
ever finished first?
Does doubt ever really rouse the rabble?
Only hatred has just what it takes.

Gifted, diligent, hardworking.
Need we mention all the songs it has composed?
All the pages it has added to our history books?
All the human carpets it has spread
over countless city squares and football fields?

Let's face it:
it knows how to make beauty.
The splendid fire-glow in midnight skies.
Magnificent bursting bombs in rosy dawns.
You can't deny the inspiring pathos of ruins
and a certain bawdy humor to be found
in the sturdy column jutting from their midst.

Hatred is a master of contrast—
between explosions and dead quiet,
red blood and white snow.
Above all, it never tires
of its leitmotif—the impeccable executioner
towering over its soiled victim.

It's always ready for new challenges.
If it has to wait awhile, it will.
They say it's blind. Blind?
It has a sniper's keen sight
and gazes unflinchingly at the future
as only it can.

Reality Demands

Reality demands
that we also mention this:
Life goes on.
It continues at Cannae and Borodino,
at Kosovo Polje and Guernica.

There's a gas station
on a little square in Jericho,
and wet paint
on park benches in Bila Hora.
Letters fly back and forth
between Pearl Harbor and Hastings,
a moving van passes
beneath the eye of the lion at Chaeronea,
and the blooming orchards near Verdun
cannot escape
the approaching atmospheric front.

There is so much Everything
that Nothing is hidden quite nicely.
Music pours
from the yachts moored at Actium
and couples dance on their sunlit decks.

So much is always going on
that it must be going on all over.
Where not a stone still stands,
you see the Ice Cream Man
besieged by children.
Where Hiroshima had been,
Hiroshima is again,

producing many products
for everyday use.

This terrifying world is not devoid of charms,
of the mornings
that make waking up worthwhile.

The grass is green
on Maciejowice's fields,
and it is studded with dew,
as is normal with grass.

Perhaps all fields are battlefields,
those we remember
and those that are forgotten:
the birch forests and the cedar forests,
the snow and the sand, the iridescent swamps
and the canyons of black defeat,
where now, when the need strikes, you don't cower
under a bush but squat behind it.

What moral flows from this? Probably none.
Only the blood flows, drying quickly,
and, as always, a few rivers, a few clouds.

On tragic mountain passes
the wind rips hats from unwitting heads
and we can't help
laughing at that.

The Real World

The real world doesn't take flight
the way dreams do.
No muffled voice, no doorbell
can dispel it,
no shriek, no crash
can cut it short.

Images in dreams
are hazy and ambiguous,
and can generally be explained
in many different ways.
Reality means reality:
that's a tougher nut to crack.

Dreams have keys.
The real world opens on its own
and can't be shut.
Report cards and stars
pour from it,
butterflies and flatiron warmers
shower down,
headless caps
and shards of clouds.
Together they form a rebus
that can't be solved.

Without us dreams couldn't exist.
The one on whom the real world depends
is still unknown,
and the products of his insomnia

are available to anyone
who wakes up.

Dreams aren't crazy—
it's the real world that's insane,
if only in the stubbornness
with which it sticks
to the current of events.

In dreams our recently deceased
are still alive,
in perfect health, no less,
and restored to the full bloom of youth.
The real world lays the corpse
in front of us.
The real world doesn't blink an eye.

Dreams are featherweights,
and memory can shake them off with ease.
The real world doesn't have to fear forgetfulness.
It's a tough customer.
It sits on our shoulders,
weighs on our hearts,
tumbles to our feet.

There's no escaping it,
it tags along each time we flee.
And there's no stop
along our escape route
where reality isn't expecting us.

Elegiac Calculation

How many of those I knew
(if I really knew them),
men, women
(if the distinction still holds)
have crossed that threshold
(if it is a threshold)
passed over that bridge
(if you can call it a bridge) —

How many, after a shorter or longer life
(if they still see a difference),
good, because it's beginning,
bad, because it's over
(if they don't prefer the reverse),
have found themselves on the far shore
(if they found themselves at all
and if another shore exists) —

I've been given no assurance
as concerns their future fate
(if there is one common fate
and if it is still fate) —

It's all
(if that word's not too confining)
behind them now
(if not before them) —

How many of them leaped from rushing time
and vanished, ever more mournfully, in the distance
(if you put stock in perspective) –

How many
(if the question makes sense,
if one can verify a final sum
without including oneself)
have sunk into that deepest sleep
(if there's nothing deeper) –

See you soon.
See you tomorrow.
See you next time.
They don't want
(if they don't want) to say that anymore.
They've given themselves up to endless
(if not otherwise) silence.
They're only concerned with that
(if only that)
which their absence demands.

Cat in an Empty Apartment

Die — you can't do that to a cat.
Since what can a cat do
in an empty apartment?
Climb the walls?
Rub up against the furniture?
Nothing seems different here,
but nothing is the same.
Nothing has been moved,
but there's more space.
And at nighttime no lamps are lit.

Footsteps on the staircase,
but they're new ones.
The hand that puts fish on the saucer
has changed, too.

Something doesn't start
at its usual time.
Something doesn't happen
as it should.
Someone was always, always here,
then suddenly disappeared
and stubbornly stays disappeared.

Every closet has been examined.
Every shelf has been explored.
Excavations under the carpet turned up nothing.
A commandment was even broken:
papers scattered everywhere.
What remains to be done.
Just sleep and wait.

Just wait till he turns up,
just let him show his face.
Will he ever get a lesson
on what not to do to a cat.
Sidle toward him
as if unwilling
and ever so slow
on visibly offended paws,
and no leaps or squeals at least to start.

Parting with a View

I don't reproach the spring
for starting up again.
I can't blame it
for doing what it must
year after year.

I know that my grief
will not stop the green.
The grass blade may bend
but only in the wind.

It doesn't pain me to see
that clumps of alders above the water
have something to rustle with again.

I take note of the fact
that the shore of a certain lake
is still — as if you were living —
as lovely as before.

I don't resent
the view for its vista
of a sun-dazzled bay.

I am even able to imagine
some non-us
sitting at this minute
on a fallen birch trunk.

I respect their right
to whisper, laugh,
and lapse into happy silence.

I can even allow
that they are bound by love
and that he holds her
with a living arm.

Something freshly birdish
starts rustling in the reeds.
I sincerely want them
to hear it.

I don't require changes
from the surf,
now diligent, now sluggish,
obeying not me.

I expect nothing
from the depths near the woods,
first emerald,
then sapphire,
then black.

There's one thing I won't agree to:
my own return.
The privilege of presence —
I give it up.

I survived you by enough,
and only by enough,
to contemplate from afar.

Séance

Happenstance reveals its tricks.
It produces, by sleight of hand, a glass of brandy
and sits Henry down beside it.
I enter the bistro and stop dead in my tracks.
Henry—he's none other than
Agnes's husband's brother,
and Agnes is related
to Aunt Sophie's brother-in-law.
It turns out
we've got the same great-grandfather.

In happenstance's hands
space furls and unfurls,
spreads and shrinks.
The tablecloth
becomes a handkerchief.
Just guess who I ran into
in Canada, of all places,
after all these years.
I thought he was dead,
and there he was, in a Mercedes.
On the plane to Athens.
At a stadium in Tokyo.

Happenstance twirls a kaleidoscope in its hands.
A billion bits of colored glass glitter.
And suddenly Jack's glass
bumps into Jill's.
Just imagine, in this very same hotel.
I turn around and see—

it's really she!
Face to face in an elevator.
In a toy store.
At the corner of Maple and Pine.

Happenstance is shrouded in a cloak.
Things get lost in it and then are found again.
I stumbled on it accidentally.
I bent down and picked it up.
One look and I knew it,
a spoon from that stolen service.
If it hadn't been for that bracelet,
I would never have known Alexandra.
The clock? It turned up in Potterville.

Happenstance looks deep into our eyes.
Our head grows heavy.
Our eyelids drop.
We want to laugh and cry,
it's so incredible.
From fourth-grade homeroom to that ocean liner.
It has to mean something.
To hell and back,
and here we meet halfway home.
We want to shout:
Small world!
You could almost hug it!
And for a moment we are filled with joy,
radiant and deceptive.

Love at First Sight

They're both convinced
that a sudden passion joined them.
Such certainty is beautiful,
but uncertainty is more beautiful still.

Since they'd never met before, they're sure
that there'd been nothing between them.
But what's the word from the streets, staircases, hallways —
perhaps they've passed by each other a million times?

I want to ask them
if they don't remember —
a moment face to face
in some revolving door?
perhaps a "sorry" muttered in a crowd?
a curt "wrong number" caught in the receiver? —
but I know the answer.
No, they don't remember.

They'd be amazed to hear
that Chance has been toying with them
now for years.

Not quite ready yet
to become their Destiny,
it pushed them close, drove them apart,
it barred their path,
stifling a laugh,
and then leaped aside.

There were signs and signals,
even if they couldn't read them yet.
Perhaps three years ago
or just last Tuesday
a certain leaf fluttered
from one shoulder to another?
Something was dropped and then picked up.
Who knows, maybe the ball that vanished
into childhood's thicket?

There were doorknobs and doorbells
where one touch had covered another
beforehand.
Suitcases checked and standing side by side.
One night, perhaps, the same dream,
grown hazy by morning.

Every beginning
is only a sequel, after all,
and the book of events
is always open halfway through.

May 16, 1973

One of those many dates
that no longer ring a bell.

Where I was going that day,
what I was doing — I don't know.

Whom I met, what we talked about,
I can't recall.

If a crime had been committed nearby,
I wouldn't have had an alibi.

The sun flared and died
beyond my horizons.
The earth rotated
unnoted in my notebooks.

I'd rather think
that I'd temporarily died
than that I kept on living
and can't remember a thing.

I wasn't a ghost, after all.
I breathed, I ate,
I walked.
My steps were audible,
my fingers surely left
their prints on doorknobs.

Mirrors caught my reflection.
I wore something or other in such-and-such a color.
Somebody must have seen me.

Maybe I found something that day
that had been lost.
Maybe I lost something that turned up later.

I was filled with feelings and sensations.
Now all that's like
a line of dots in parentheses.

Where was I hiding out,
where did I bury myself?
Not a bad trick
to vanish before my own eyes.

I shake my memory.
Maybe something in its branches
that has been asleep for years
will start up with a flutter.

No.
Clearly I'm asking too much.
Nothing less than one whole second.

Maybe All This

Maybe all this
is happening in some lab?
Under one lamp by day
and billions by night?

Maybe we're experimental generations?
Poured from one vial to the next,
shaken in test tubes,
not scrutinized by eyes alone,
each of us separately
plucked up by tweezers in the end?

Or maybe it's more like this:
No interference?
The changes occur on their own
according to plan?
The graph's needle slowly etches
its predictable zigzags?

Maybe thus far we aren't of much interest?
The control monitors aren't usually plugged in?
Only for wars, preferably large ones,
for the odd ascent above our clump of Earth,
for major migrations from point A to B?

Maybe just the opposite:
They've got a taste for trivia up there?
Look! on the big screen a little girl
is sewing a button on her sleeve.
The radar shrieks,
the staff comes at a run.
What a darling little being
with its tiny heart beating inside it!
How sweet, its solemn
threading of the needle!
Someone cries enraptured:
Get the Boss,
tell him he's got to see this for himself!

Slapstick

If there are angels,
I doubt they read
our novels
concerning thwarted hopes.

I'm afraid, alas,
they never touch the poems
that bear our grudges against the world.

The rantings and railings
of our plays
must drive them, I suspect,
to distraction.

Off duty, between angelic —
i.e., inhuman — occupations,
they watch instead
our slapstick
from the age of silent film.

To our dirge wailers,
garment renders,
and teeth gnashers,
they prefer, I suppose,
that poor devil
who grabs the drowning man by his toupee
or, starving, devours his own shoelaces
with gusto.

From the waist up, starch and aspirations;
below, a startled mouse
runs down his trousers.
I'm sure
that's what they call real entertainment.

A crazy chase in circles
ends up pursuing the pursuer.
The light at the end of the tunnel
turns out to be a tiger's eye.
A hundred disasters
mean a hundred comic somersaults
turned over a hundred abysses.

If there are angels,
they must, I hope,
find this convincing,
this merriment dangling from terror,
not even crying Save me Save me
since all of this takes place in silence.

I can even imagine
that they clap their wings
and tears run from their eyes
from laughter, if nothing else.

Nothing's a Gift

Nothing's a gift, it's all on loan.
I'm drowning in debts up to my ears.
I'll have to pay for myself
with my self,
give up my life for my life.

Here's how it's arranged:
The heart can be repossessed,
the liver, too,
and each single finger and toe.

Too late to tear up the terms,
my debts will be repaid,
and I'll be fleeced,
or, more precisely, flayed.

I move about the planet
in a crush of other debtors.
Some are saddled with the burden
of paying off their wings.
Others must, willy-nilly,
account for every leaf.

Every tissue in us lies
on the debit side.
Not a tentacle or tendril
is for keeps.

The inventory, infinitely detailed,
implies we'll be left
not just empty-handed
but handless, too.

I can't remember
where, when, and why
I let someone open
this account in my name.

We call the protest against this
the soul.
And it's the only item
not included on the list.

One Version of Events

If we'd been allowed to choose,
we'd probably have gone on forever.

The bodies that were offered didn't fit,
and wore out horribly.

The ways of sating hunger
made us sick.
We were repelled
by blind heredity
and the tyranny of glands.

The world that was meant to embrace us
decayed without end
and the effects of causes raged over it.

Individual fates
were presented for our inspection:
appalled and grieved,
we rejected most of them.

Questions naturally arose, e.g.,
who needs the painful birth
of a dead child,
and what's in it for a sailor
who will never reach the shore.

We agreed to death,
but not to every kind.
Love attracted us,
of course, but only love
that keeps its word.

Both fickle standards
and the impermanence of artworks
kept us wary of the Muses' service.

Each of us wished to have a homeland
free of neighbors
and to live his entire life
in the intervals between wars.

No one wished to seize power
or to be subject to it.
No one wanted to fall victim
to his own or others' delusions.
No one volunteered
for crowd scenes and processions,
to say nothing of dying tribes —
although without all these
history couldn't run its charted course
through centuries to come.

Meanwhile, a fair number
of stars lit earlier
had died out and grown cold.
It was high time for a decision.

Voicing numerous reservations,
candidates finally emerged
for a number of roles as healers and explorers,
a few obscure philosophers,
one or two nameless gardeners,
artists and virtuosos —

though even these livings
couldn't all be filled
for lack of other kinds of applications.

It was time to think
the whole thing over.

We'd been offered a trip
from which we'd surely be returning soon,
wouldn't we.

A trip outside eternity—
monotonous, no matter what they say,
and foreign to time's flow.
The chance may never come our way again.

We were besieged by doubts.
Does knowing everything beforehand
really mean knowing everything.

Is a decision made in advance
really any kind of choice.
Wouldn't we be better off
dropping the subject
and making our minds up
once we get there.

We looked at the earth.
Some daredevils were already living there.

A feeble weed
clung to a rock,
trusting blindly
that the wind wouldn't tear it off.

A small animal
dug itself from its burrow
with an energy and hope
that puzzled us.

We struck ourselves as prudent,
petty, and ridiculous.

In any case, our ranks began to dwindle.
The most impatient of us disappeared.
They'd left for the first trial by fire,
this much was clear,
especially by the glare of the real fire
they'd just begun to light
on the steep bank of an actual river.

A few of them
have actually turned back.
But not in our direction.
And with something they seemed to have won in their hands.

We're Extremely Fortunate

We're extremely fortunate
not to know precisely
the kind of world we live in.

One would have
to live a long, long time,
unquestionably longer
than the world itself.

Get to know other worlds,
if only for comparison.

Rise above the flesh,
which only really knows
how to obstruct
and make trouble.

For the sake of research,
the big picture
and definitive conclusions,
one would have to transcend time,
in which everything scurries and whirls.

From that perspective,
one might as well bid farewell
to incidents and details.

The counting of weekdays
would inevitably seem to be
a senseless activity;

dropping letters in the mailbox
a whim of foolish youth;

the sign "No Walking on the Grass"
a symptom of lunacy.

MOMENT

2002

Moment

I walk on the slope of a hill gone green.
Grass, little flowers in the grass,
as in a children's illustration.
The misty sky's already turning blue.
A view of other hills unfolds in silence.

As if there'd never been any Cambrians, Silurians,
rocks snarling at crags,
upturned abysses,
no nights in flames
and days in clouds of darkness.

As if plains hadn't pushed their way here
in malignant fevers,
icy shivers.

As if seas had seethed only elsewhere,
shredding the shores of the horizons.

It's nine thirty local time.
Everything's in its place and in polite agreement.
In the valley a little brook cast as a little brook.
A path in the role of a path from always to ever.
Woods disguised as woods alive without end,
and above them birds in flight play birds in flight.

This moment reigns as far as the eye can reach.
One of those earthly moments
invited to linger.

Among the Multitudes

I am who I am.
A coincidence no less unthinkable
than any other.

I could have had different
ancestors, after all.
I could have fluttered
from another nest
or crawled bescaled
from under another tree.

Nature's wardrobe
holds a fair supply of costumes:
spider, seagull, field mouse.
Each fits perfectly right off
and is dutifully worn
into shreds.

I didn't get a choice either,
but I can't complain.
I could have been someone
much less separate.
Someone from an anthill, shoal, or buzzing swarm,
an inch of landscape tousled by the wind.

Someone much less fortunate
bred for my fur
or Christmas dinner,
something swimming under a square of glass.

A tree rooted to the ground
as the fire draws near.

A grass blade trampled by a stampede
of incomprehensible events.

A shady type whose darkness
dazzled some.

What if I'd prompted only fear,
loathing,
or pity?

If I'd been born
in the wrong tribe,
with all roads closed before me?

Fate has been kind
to me thus far.

I might never have been given
the memory of happy moments.

My yen for comparison
might have been taken away.

I might have been myself minus amazement,
that is,
someone completely different.

Clouds

I'd have to be really quick
to describe clouds –
a split second's enough
for them to start being something else.

Their trademark:
they don't repeat a single
shape, shade, pose, arrangement.

Unburdened by memory of any kind,
they float easily over the facts.

What on earth could they bear witness to?
They scatter whenever something happens.

Compared to clouds,
life rests on solid ground,
practically permanent, almost eternal.

Next to clouds
even a stone seems like a brother,
someone you can trust,
while they're just distant, flighty cousins.

Let people exist if they want,
and then die, one after another:
clouds simply don't care
what they're up to
down there.

And so their haughty fleet
cruises smoothly over your whole life
and mine, still incomplete.

They aren't obliged to vanish when we're gone.
They don't have to be seen while sailing on.

Negative

Against a grayish sky
a grayer cloud
rimmed black by the sun.

On the left, that is, the right,
a white cherry branch with black blossoms.

Light shadows on your dark face.
You'd just taken a seat at the table
and put your hands, gone gray, upon it.

You look like a ghost
who's trying to summon up the living.

(And since I still number among them,
I should appear to him and tap:
good night, that is, good morning,
farewell, that is, hello.
And not grudge questions to any of his answers
concerning life,
that storm before the calm.)

Receiver

I dream that I'm woken
by the telephone.

I dream the certainty
that someone dead is calling.

I dream that I reach
for the receiver.

Only the receiver's
not how it used to be,
it's gotten heavy
as if it had grabbed onto something,
grown into something,
and wrapped its roots around it.
I'd have to rip the whole Earth
out with it.

I dream my useless
struggles.

I dream the quiet,
since the ringing's stopped.

I dream I fall asleep
and wake up again.

The Three Oddest Words

When I pronounce the word Future,
the first syllable already belongs to the past.

When I pronounce the word Silence,
I destroy it.

When I pronounce the word Nothing,
I make something no nonbeing can hold.

The Silence of Plants

Our one-sided acquaintance
grows quite nicely.

I know what a leaf, petal, ear, cone, stalk is,
what April and December do to you.

Although my curiosity is not reciprocal,
I specially stoop over some of you,
and crane my neck at others.

I've got a list of names for you:
maple, burdock, hepatica,
mistletoe, heath, juniper, forget-me-not,
but you have none for me.

We're traveling together.
But fellow passengers usually chat,
exchange remarks at least about the weather,
or about the stations rushing past.

We wouldn't lack for topics: we've got a lot in common.
The same star keeps us in its reach.
We cast shadows based on the same laws.
We try to understand things, each in our own way,
and what we don't know brings us closer too.

I'll explain as best I can, just ask me:
what seeing with two eyes is like,
what my heart beats for,
and why my body isn't rooted down.

But how to answer unasked questions,
while being furthermore a being so totally
a nobody to you.

Undergrowth, coppices, meadows, rushes —
everything I tell you is a monologue,
and it's not you who listens.

Talking with you is essential and impossible.
Urgent in this hurried life
and postponed to never.

Plato, or Why

For unclear reasons
under unknown circumstances
Ideal Being ceased to be satisfied.

It could have gone on forever,
hewn from darkness, forged from light,
in its sleepy gardens above the world.

Why on earth did it start seeking thrills
in the bad company of matter?

What use could it have for imitators,
inept, ill-starred,
lacking all prospects for eternity?

Wisdom limping
with a thorn stuck in its heel?
Harmony derailed
by roiling waters?
Beauty
holding unappealing entrails
and Good —
why the shadow
when it didn't have one before?

There must have been some reason,
however slight,
but even the Naked Truth, busy ransacking
the earth's wardrobe,
won't betray it.

Not to mention, Plato, those appalling poets,
litter scattered by the breeze from under statues,
scraps from that great Silence up on high . . .

A Little Girl Tugs at the Tablecloth

She's been in this world for over a year,
and in this world not everything's been examined
and taken in hand.

The subject of today's investigation
is things that don't move by themselves.

They need to be helped along,
shoved, shifted,
taken from their place and relocated.

They don't all want to go, e.g., the bookshelf,
the cupboard, the unyielding walls, the table.

But the tablecloth on the stubborn table
— when well seized by its hems —
manifests a willingness to travel.

And the glasses, plates,
creamer, spoons, bowl,
are fairly shaking with desire.

It's fascinating,
what form of motion will they take,
once they're trembling on the brink:
will they roam across the ceiling?
fly around the lamp?
hop onto the windowsill and from there to a tree?

Mr. Newton still has no say in this.
Let him look down from the heavens and wave his hand.

This experiment must be completed.
And it will.

A Memory

We were chatting
and suddenly stopped short.
A lovely girl stepped onto the terrace,
so lovely,
too lovely
for us to enjoy our trip.

Basia shot her husband a stricken look.
Krystyna took Zbyszek's hand
reflexively.
I thought: I'll call you,
tell you, don't come just yet,
they're predicting rain for days.

Only Agnieszka, a widow,
met the lovely girl with a smile.

Puddle

I remember that childhood fear well.
I avoided puddles,
especially fresh ones, after showers.
One of them might be bottomless, after all,
even though it looks just like the rest.

I'll step and suddenly be swallowed whole,
I'll start rising downward,
then even deeper down
toward the reflected clouds
and maybe farther.

Then the puddle will dry up,
shut above me,
I'm trapped for good — where —
with a shout that never made it to the surface.

Understanding came only later:
not all misadventures
fit within the world's laws
and even if they wanted to,
they couldn't happen.

First Love

They say
the first love's most important.
That's very romantic,
but not my experience.

Something was and wasn't there between us,
something went on and went away.

My hands never tremble
when I stumble on silly keepsakes
and a sheaf of letters tied with string
— not even ribbon.

Our only meeting after years:
two chairs chatting
at a chilly table.

Other loves
still breathe deep inside me.
This one's too short of breath even to sigh.

Yet just exactly as it is,
it does what the others still can't manage:
unremembered,
not even seen in dreams,
it introduces me to death.

A Few Words on the Soul

We have a soul at times.
No one's got it nonstop,
for keeps.

Day after day,
year after year
may pass without it.

Sometimes
it will settle for a while
only in childhood's fears and raptures.
Sometimes only in astonishment
that we are old.

It rarely lends a hand
in uphill tasks,
like moving furniture,
or lifting luggage,
or going miles in shoes that pinch.

It usually steps out
whenever meat needs chopping
or forms have to be filled.

For every thousand conversations
it participates in one,
if even that,
since it prefers silence.

Just when our body goes from ache to pain,
it slips off duty.

It's picky:
it doesn't like seeing us in crowds,
our hustling for a dubious advantage
and creaky machinations make it sick.

Joy and sorrow
aren't two different feelings for it.
It attends us
only when the two are joined.

We can count on it
when we're sure of nothing
and curious about everything.

Among the material objects
it favors clocks with pendulums
and mirrors, which keep on working
even when no one is looking.

It won't say where it comes from
or when it's taking off again,
though it's clearly expecting such questions.

We need it
but apparently
it needs us
for some reason too.

Early Hour

I'm still asleep,
but meanwhile facts are taking place.
The window grows white,
darknesses turn gray,
the room works its way from hazy space,
pale, shaky stripes seek its support.

By turns, unhurried,
since this is a ceremony,
the planes of walls and ceiling dawn,
shapes separate,
one from the other,
left to right.

The distances between objects irradiate,
the first glints twitter
on the tumbler, the doorknob.
Whatever had been displaced yesterday,
had fallen to the floor,
been contained in picture frames,
is no longer simply happening, but is.
Only the details
have not yet entered the field of vision.

But look out, look out, look out,
all indicators point to returning colors
and even the smallest thing regains its own hue
along with a hint of shadow.

This rarely astounds me, but it should.
I usually wake up in the role of belated witness,
with the miracle already achieved,
the day defined
and dawning masterfully recast as morning.

In the Park

—Hey! the little boy wonders,
who's that lady?

—It's a statue of Charity,
something like that,
his mother answers.

—But how come that lady's
so-o-o-o beat-up?

—I don't know, she's always
been like that, I think.
The city should do something about it.
Get rid of it, fix it.
Well, don't dawdle, let's get going.

A Contribution to Statistics

Out of a hundred people

those who always know better
— fifty-two,

doubting every step
— nearly all the rest,

glad to lend a hand
if it doesn't take too long
— as high as forty-nine,

always good
because they can't be otherwise
— four, well, maybe five,

able to admire without envy
— eighteen,

living in constant fear
of someone or something
— seventy-seven,

capable of happiness
— twenty-something tops,

harmless singly,
savage in crowds
— half at least,

cruel
when forced by circumstances
— better not to know
even ballpark figures,

wise after the fact
—just a couple more
than wise before it,

taking only things from life
—forty
(I wish I were wrong),

hunched in pain,
no flashlight in the dark
—eighty-three
sooner or later,

worthy of compassion
—ninety-nine,

mortal
—a hundred out of a hundred.
Thus far this figure still remains unchanged.

Some People

Some people flee some other people.
In some country under a sun
and some clouds.

They abandon something close to all they've got,
sown fields, some chickens, dogs,
mirrors in which fire now preens.

Their shoulders bear pitchers and bundles.
The emptier they get, the heavier they grow.

What happens quietly: someone's dropping from exhaustion.
What happens loudly: someone's bread is ripped away,
someone tries to shake a limp child back to life.

Always another wrong road ahead of them,
always another wrong bridge
across an oddly reddish river.
Around them, some gunshots, now nearer, now farther away,
above them a plane seems to circle.

Some invisibility would come in handy,
some grayish stoniness,
or, better yet, some nonexistence
for a shorter or a longer while.

Something else will happen, only where and what.
Someone will come at them, only when and who,
in how many shapes, with what intentions.
If he has a choice,
maybe he won't be the enemy
and will let them live some sort of life.

Photograph from September 11

They jumped from the burning floors —
one, two, a few more,
higher, lower.

The photograph halted them in life,
and now keeps them
above the earth toward the earth.

Each is still complete,
with a particular face
and blood well hidden.

There's enough time
for hair to come loose,
for keys and coins
to fall from pockets.

They're still within the air's reach,
within the compass of places
that have just now opened.

I can do only two things for them —
describe this flight
and not add a last line.

Return Baggage

The cemetery plot for tiny graves.
We, the long lived, pass by furtively,
like wealthy people passing slums.

Here lie little Zosia, Jacek, Dominik,
prematurely stripped of the sun, the moon,
the clouds, the turning seasons.

They didn't stash much in their return bags.
Some scraps of sights
that scarcely count as plural.
A fistful of air with a butterfly flitting.
A spoonful of bitter knowledge — the taste of medicine.

Small-scale naughtiness,
granted, some of it fatal.
Gaily chasing the ball across the road.
The happiness of skating on thin ice.

This one here, that one down there, those on the end:
before they grew to reach a doorknob,
break a watch,
smash their first windowpane.

Malgorzata, four years old,
two of them spent staring at the ceiling.

Rafalek: missed his fifth birthday by a month,
and Zuzia missed Christmas,
when misty breath turns to frost.

And what can you say about one day of life,
a minute, a second:
darkness, a lightbulb's flash, then dark again?

KOSMOS MAKROS
CHRONOS PARADOKSOS
Only stony Greek has words for that.

The Ball

As long as nothing can be known for sure,
(no signals have been picked up yet),

as long as Earth is still unlike
the nearer and more distant planets,

as long as there's neither hide nor hair
of other grasses graced by other winds,
of other treetops bearing other crowns,
other animals as well grounded as our own,

as long as only the local echo
has been known to speak in syllables,

as long as there's still no word
of better or worse mozarts,
platos, edisons out there,

as long as our inhuman crimes
are still committed only among humans,

as long as our kindness
is still incomparable,
peerless even in its imperfection,

as long as our heads packed with illusions
still pass for the only heads so packed,

as long as the roofs of our mouths alone
still raise voices to high heavens —

let's act like very special guests of honor
at the district fireman's ball,
dance to the beat of the local oompah band,
and pretend that it's the ball
to end all balls.

I can't speak for others —
for me this is
misery and happiness enough:

just this sleepy backwater
where even the stars have time to burn
while winking at us
unintentionally.

A Note

Life is the only way
to get covered in leaves,
catch your breath on the sand,
rise on wings;

to be a dog,
or stroke its warm fur;

to tell pain
from everything it's not;

to squeeze inside events,
dawdle in views,
to seek the least of all possible mistakes.

An extraordinary chance
to remember for a moment
a conversation held
with the lamp switched off;

and if only once
to stumble on a stone,
end up drenched in one downpour or another,

mislay your keys in the grass;
and to follow a spark on the wind with your eyes;

and to keep on not knowing
something important.

List

I've made a list of questions
to which I no longer expect answers,
since it's either too early for them,
or I won't have time to understand.

The list of questions is long,
and takes up matters great and small,
but I don't want to bore you,
and will just divulge a few:

What was real
and what scarcely seemed to be
in this auditorium,
stellar and substellar,
requiring tickets for entrance
and exit alike;

What about the whole live world,
which I won't manage
to compare with any other living world;

What will the papers
write about tomorrow;

When will wars cease,
and what will replace them;

Whose third finger now wears
the ring
stolen from me — lost;

What's the place of free will,
which manages to be and not to be
simultaneously;

What about those scores of people —
did we really know each other;

What was M. trying to tell me
when she could no longer speak;

Why did I take bad things
for good ones
and what would it take
to keep from doing it again?

There are certain questions
I jotted down just before sleep.
On waking
I couldn't make them out.

Sometimes I suspect
that it's a real code,
but that question, too,
will take its leave one day.

Everything

Everything —
a smug and bumptious word.
It should be written in quotes.
It pretends to miss nothing,
to gather, hold, contain, and have.
While all the while it's just
a shred of gale.

COLON

2005

Absence

A few minor changes
and my mother might have married
Mr. Zbigniew B. from Zduńska Wola.
And if they'd had a daughter — she wouldn't have been me.
Maybe with a better memory for names and faces,
and any melody heard once.
Adept at telling one bird from another.
With perfect grades in chemistry and physics,
and worse in Polish,
but secretly writing poems
instantly more interesting than mine.

A few minor changes
and my father might at that same time have married
Miss Jadwiga R. from Zakopane.
And if they'd had a daughter — she wouldn't have been me.
Maybe standing her ground more stubbornly.
Plunging headfirst into deep water.
Susceptible to group emotions.
Always seen in several spots at once,
but rarely with a book, more often in the yard
playing kickball with the boys.

They might even have met
in the same school, the same room.
But not kindred spirits,
no affinities,
at opposite ends of class photos.

Stand here, girls
— the photographer would call —

shorter girls in front, tall girls behind.
And big smiles when I say cheese.
But one more head count,
that's everyone?

— Yes sir, that's all.

ABC

I'll never find out now
what A. thought of me.
If B. ever forgave me in the end.
Why C. pretended everything was fine.
What part D. played in E.'s silence.
What F. had been expecting, if anything.
Why G. forgot when she knew perfectly well.
What H. had to hide.
What I. wanted to add.
If my being nearby
meant anything
for J. and K. and the rest of the alphabet.

Highway Accident

They still don't know
what happened on the highway
half an hour ago.

On their watches
it's just the same old time,
afternoonish, Thursdayish, September.

Someone is draining macaroni.
Someone is raking leaves.
Squealing children race around the table.
Someone's cat deigns to be patted.
Someone is crying—
as always when bad Diego
betrays Juanita on TV.
Someone is knocking—
nothing, the neighbor with a borrowed frying pan.
A phone rings deep in the apartment—
just telemarketing for now.

If someone were to stand at the window
and look out at the sky,
he might catch sight of clouds
drifting over from the accident.
Torn and tattered, to be sure,
but that's business as usual for them.

The Day After — Without Us

The morning is expected to be cool and foggy.
Rainclouds
will move in from the west.
Poor visibility.
Slick highways.

Gradually as the day progresses
high pressure fronts from the north
make local sunshine likely.
Due to winds, though, sometimes strong and gusty,
sun may give way to storms.

At night
clearing across the country,
with a slight chance of precipitation
only in the southeast.
Temperatures will drop sharply,
while barometric readings rise.

The next day
promises to be sunny,
although those still living
should bring umbrellas.

An Occurrence

Sky, earth, morning,
the time is eight fifteen.
Peace and quiet
in the savanna's yellowed grass.
An ebony tree in the distance
with evergreen leaves
and spreading roots.

A sudden uproar in the blissful stillness.
Two creatures who want to live suddenly bolt.
An antelope in violent flight,
a breathless hungry lioness behind her.
Their chances are equal for the moment.
The antelope may even have the edge.
And if not for the root
that thrusts from the ground,
if not for the stumble
of one of four hooves,
if not for the split second
of disrupted rhythm
that the lioness seizes
with one prolonged leap —

On the question of guilt,
nothing, only silence.
The sky, *circulus coelestis,* is innocent.
Terra nutrix, breadwinner earth, is innocent.
Tempus fugitivum, time, is innocent.
The antelope, *gazella dorcas,* is innocent.
The lioness, *leo massaicus,* is innocent.
The ebony tree, *diospyros mespiliformis,* is innocent.
And the observer who watches through binoculars
is, in such instances,
homo sapiens innocens.

Consolation

Darwin.
They say he read novels to relax.
But only certain kinds:
nothing that ended unhappily.
If he happened on something like that,
enraged, he flung the book into the fire.

True or not,
I'm ready to believe it.

Scanning in his mind so many times and places,
he'd had enough of dying species,
the triumphs of the strong over the weak,
the endless struggles to survive,
all doomed sooner or later.
He'd earned the right to happy endings,
at least in fiction
with its microscales.

Hence the indispensable silver lining,
the lovers reunited, the families reconciled,
the doubts dispelled, fidelity rewarded,
fortunes regained, treasures uncovered,
stiff-necked neighbors mending their ways,
good names restored, greed daunted,
old maids married off to worthy parsons,
troublemakers banished to other hemispheres,
forgers of documents tossed down the stairs,

seducers scurrying to the altar,
orphans sheltered, widows comforted,
pride humbled, wounds healed,
prodigal sons summoned home,
cups of sorrow tossed into the ocean,
hankies drenched with tears of reconciliation,
general merriment and celebration,
and the dog Fido,
gone astray in the first chapter,
turns up barking gladly
in the last.

The Old Professor

I asked him about the old days,
when we were still so young,
naïve, hotheaded, silly, green.

Some of that remains, except the young part,
he replied.

I asked if he still knew for sure
what was good and bad for humankind.

The most deadly of all illusions,
he replied.

I asked about the future,
did he still see it clearly.

I've read too many history books,
he replied.

I asked about the photo,
the framed one, on his desk.

Here and gone. Brother, cousin, sister-in-law,
my wife, my daughter on her lap,
the cat in my daughter's arms,
and the cherry tree blossoming, and above it
an unidentified bird flying
—he replied.

I asked if he was happy sometimes.

I work,
he replied.

I asked about his friends, did he still have them.

A few former assistants,
who have their own former assistants,
Ludmila, who looks after the house,
someone very close, but far away,
two ladies from the library, both smiling,
little Grześ across the hall and Marcus Aurelius,
he replied.

I asked about his health, his state of mind.

They won't give me coffee, vodka, cigarettes,
won't let me carry heavy memories and objects.
I just pretend that I can't hear them
—he replied.

I asked about the garden and the garden bench.

When the night is clear, I watch the sky.
I can't get enough of it,
so many points of view,
he replied.

Perspective

They passed like strangers,
without a word or gesture,
she off to the store,
he heading to his car.

Were they panicked
or distracted,
or forgetting
that for a little while
they'd been in love forever.

There's no guarantee, though,
that it was them.
Maybe at a distance
but not close up.

I watched them from a window,
but observers from above
are easily mistaken.

She vanished behind glass doors,
he sat behind the wheel
and took off.
Nothing happened, that is,
even if it did.

But sure of what I'd seen
just for a moment,
I try in this chance poem
to persuade you, oh readers,
it was sad.

The Courtesy of the Blind

The poet reads his lines to the blind.
He hadn't guessed that it would be so hard.
His voice trembles.
His hands shake.

He senses that every sentence
is put to the test of darkness.
He must muddle through alone,
without colors or lights.

A treacherous endeavor
for his poems' stars,
dawns, rainbows, clouds, their neon lights, their moon,
for the fish so silvery thus far beneath the water
and the hawk so high and quiet in the sky.

He reads — since it's too late to stop now —
about the boy in a yellow jacket on a green field,
red roofs that can be counted in the valley,
the restless numbers on soccer players' shirts,
and the naked stranger standing in a half-shut door.

He'd like to skip — although it can't be done —
all the saints on that cathedral ceiling,
the parting wave from a train,
the microscope lens, the ring casting a glow,
the movie screens, the mirrors, the photo albums.

But great is the courtesy of the blind,
great is their forbearance, their largesse.
They listen, smile, and applaud.

One of them even comes up
with a book turned wrong side out
asking for an unseen autograph.

Monologue of a Dog Ensnared in History

There are dogs and dogs. I was among the chosen.
I had good papers and wolf's blood in my veins.
I lived upon the heights inhaling the odors of views:
meadows in sunlight, spruces after rain,
and clumps of earth beneath the snow.

I had a decent home and people on call,
I was fed, washed, groomed,
and taken for lovely strolls.
Respectfully, though, and comme il faut.
They all knew full well whose dog I was.

Any lousy mutt can have a master.
Take care, though — beware comparisons.
My master was a breed apart.
He had a splendid herd that trailed his every step
and fixed its eyes on him in fearful awe.

For me they always had smiles,
with envy poorly hidden.
Since only I had the right
to greet him with nimble leaps,
only I could say goodbye by worrying his trousers with my teeth.
Only I was permitted
to receive scratching and stroking
with my head laid in his lap.
Only I could feign sleep
while he bent over me to whisper something.

He raged at others often, loudly.
He snarled, barked,
raced from wall to wall.
I suspect he liked only me
and nobody else, ever.

I also had responsibilities: waiting, trusting.
Since he would turn up briefly and then vanish.
What kept him down there in the lowlands, I don't know.
I guessed, though, it must be pressing business,
at least as pressing
as my battle with the cats
and everything that moves for no good reason.

There's fate and fate. Mine changed abruptly.
One spring came
and he wasn't there.
All hell broke loose at home.
Suitcases, chests, trunks crammed into cars.
The wheels squealed tearing downhill
and fell silent round the bend.

On the terrace scraps and tatters flamed,
yellow shirts, armbands with black emblems,
and lots and lots of battered cartons
with little banners tumbling out.

I tossed and turned in this whirlwind,
more amazed than peeved.
I felt unfriendly glances on my fur.
As if I were a dog without a master,
some pushy stray
chased downstairs with a broom.

Someone tore my silver-trimmed collar off,
someone kicked my bowl, empty for days.
Then someone else, driving away,
leaned out from the car
and shot me twice.

He couldn't even shoot straight,
since I died for a long time, in pain,
to the buzz of impertinent flies.
I, the dog of my master.

An Interview with Atropos

Madame Atropos?

That's correct.

Of Necessity's three daughters,
you fare the worst in world opinion.

A gross exaggeration, my dear poet.
Clotho spins the thread of life,
but the thread is delicate
and easily cut.
Lachesis determines its length with her rod.
They are no angels.

Still, you, madame, hold the scissors.

And since I do, I put them to good use.

I see that even as we speak . . .

I'm a Type A, that's my nature.

You don't get bored or tired,
maybe drowsy working nights? Really, not in the slightest?
With no holidays, vacations, weekends,
no quick breaks for cigarettes?

We'd fall behind, I don't like that.

Such breathtaking industry.
But you're not given commendations,
orders, trophies, cups, awards?
Maybe just a framed diploma?

Like at the hairdresser's? No, thank you.

Who, if anyone, assists you?

A tidy little paradox — you mortals.
Assorted dictators, untold fanatics.
Not that they need me to nudge them.
They're eager to get down to work.

Wars must surely make you happy,
what with all the extra help you get.

Happy? I don't know the feeling.
I'm not the one who declares them,
I'm not the one who steers their course.
I will admit, though, that I'm grateful,
they do serve to keep me au courant.

You're not sorry for the threads cut short?

A little shorter, a lot shorter —
Only you perceive the difference.

And if someone stronger wanted to relieve you,
tried to make you take retirement?

I don't follow. Express yourself more clearly.

I'll try once more: do you have a Higher-Up?

. . . *Next question please.*

That's all I've got.

Well, goodbye then.
Or to put it more precisely . . .

I know, I know. Au revoir.

The Poet's Nightmare

Just imagine what I dreamed.
Everything as if the way it is.
Ground beneath your feet, water, fire, air,
vertical, horizontal, triangle, circle,
left and right.
Reasonable weather, decent scenery,
a fair number of creatures endowed with speech.
But their speech is different than here on Earth.

Sentences are governed by the unconditional.
Names stick strictly to things.
Nothing to add, subtract, change, rearrange.

Time always by the clock.
Past and future know their place.
For remembrance a single vanished second,
for predictions a moment
that has already begun.

Words as needed. Not one more,
which means no poetry,
no philosophy, no religion.
Such follies don't come into play.

Nothing that can just be thought
or seen with eyes shut.

Search only for what's right at hand.
Ask only if there are answers.

They'd be amazed,
if they could be amazed,
that somewhere there are reasons for amazement.

The entry for "uneasy," considered lewd,
wouldn't dare to appear in their dictionaries.

The world seems clear
even in deepest darkness.
Each is charged a suitable price.
No one asks for change at the cashier's.

Among feelings – satisfaction. And no parentheses.
Life with a full stop at its heel. And the hum of galaxies.

Admit that nothing worse
could happen to a poet.
And afterward nothing better
than waking up.

Labyrinth

— and now a few steps
from wall to wall,
up those stairs
or down the others,
then slightly to the left,
if not the right,
from a wall within a wall
up to the seventh threshold,
from wherever to wherever
to the very intersection
where your hopes, errors, failures,
efforts, plans, and new hopes
cross paths
so as to part.

Road after road
without retreat.
Access only to those
you have before you,
and there, as if in consolation,
twist after twist,
gasp after gasp,
view after view.
You may choose
where to be or not to be,
to overpass or to pull over,
only not to overlook.

So this way or that,
if not the other,
by intuition, by premonition,
by common sense, by chance,
by hook or crook,
by crooked shortcuts.
Through whichever rows upon rows
of corridors and gates,
quick, since in the meantime
your time is running short,
from place to place,
to those many still left open,
where there's perplexity and darkness
but also gaps and rapture,
where there's happiness, though mishap
is just a step behind,
whereas elsewhere, hither thither,
here and there, wherever,
fortune in misfortune
like brackets in parentheses,
and yes to all of this,
then abruptly an abyss,
an abyss, but a little bridge,
a little bridge, but shaky,
shaky, but the only,
there's no other.

There must be an exit somewhere,
that's more than certain.
But you don't look for it,
it looks for you,
it's been stalking you
from the start,
and this labyrinth
is none other than
than your, for the duration,
your, until not your,
flight, flight —

Distraction

I misbehaved in the cosmos yesterday.
I lived around the clock without questions,
without surprise.

I performed daily tasks
as if only that were required.

Inhale, exhale, right foot, left, obligations,
not a thought beyond
getting there and getting back.

The world might have been taken for bedlam,
but I took it just for daily use.

No — whats — no what-fors —
and why on earth it is —
and how come it needs so many moving parts.

I was like a nail stuck only halfway in the wall
or
(comparison I couldn't find).

One change happened after another
even in a twinkling's narrow span.

Yesterday's bread was sliced otherwise
by a hand a day younger at a younger table.

Clouds like never before and rain like never,
since it fell after all in different drops.

The world rotated on its axis,
but in a space abandoned forever.

This took a good 24 hours.
1,440 minutes of opportunity.
86,400 seconds for inspection.

The cosmic savoir-vivre
may keep silent on our subject,
still it makes a few demands:
occasional attention, one or two of Pascal's thoughts,
and amazed participation in a game
with rules unknown.

Greek Statue

With the help of people and the other elements
time hasn't done a bad job on it.
It first removed the nose, then the genitalia,
next, one by one, the toes and fingers,
over the years the arms, one after the other,
the left thigh, the right,
the shoulders, hips, head, and buttocks,
and whatever dropped off has since fallen to pieces,
to rubble, to gravel, to sand.

When someone living dies that way
blood flows at every blow.

But marble statues die white
and not always completely.

From the one under discussion only the torso lingers
and it's like a breath held with great effort,
since now it must
draw
to itself
all the grace and gravity
of what was lost.

And it does,
for now it does,
it does and it dazzles,
it dazzles and endures —

Time likewise merits some applause here,
since it stopped work early,
and left some for later.

In Fact Every Poem

In fact every poem
might be called "Moment."

One phrase is enough
in the present tense,
the past and even future;

it's enough so that anything
borne on words
begins to rustle, sparkle,
flutter, float,
while seeming
to stay changeless
but with a shifting shadow;

it's enough that there is talk
of someone next to someone
or someone next to something;

about Sally who has a kitty
or no longer has a kitty;

or about other Sallys
kitties or not kitties
from other primers
ruffled by the wind;

it's enough if within eyeshot
an author places temporary hills
and makeshift valleys;

if on this occasion
he hints at a heaven
apparently firm and enduring;

if there appears beneath a writing hand
at least one thing
that is called someone's;

if in black on white,
at least in thought,
for some serious or silly reason,
question marks are placed,
and if in response,
a colon:

HERE

2009

Here

I can't speak for elsewhere,
but here on Earth we've got a fair supply of everything.
Here we manufacture chairs and sorrows,
scissors, tenderness, transistors, violins,
teacups, dams, and quips.

There may be more of everything elsewhere,
but for reasons left unspecified they lack paintings,
picture tubes, pierogies, handkerchiefs for tears.

Here we have countless places with vicinities.
You may take a liking to some,
give them pet names,
protect them from harm.

There may be comparable places elsewhere,
but no one thinks they're beautiful.

Like nowhere else, or almost nowhere,
you're given your own torso here,
equipped with the accessories required
for adding your own children to the rest.
Not to mention arms, legs, and astounded head.

Ignorance works overtime here,
something is always being counted, compared, measured,
from which roots and conclusions are then drawn.

I know, I know what you're thinking.
Nothing here can last,
since from and to time immemorial the elements hold sway.

But see, even the elements grow weary
and sometimes take extended breaks
before starting up again.

And I know what you're thinking next.
Wars, wars, wars.
But there are pauses in between them too.
Attention! — people are evil.
At ease — people are good.
At attention wastelands are created.
At ease houses are constructed in the sweat of brows,
and quickly inhabited.

Life on Earth is quite a bargain.
Dreams, for one, don't charge admission.
Illusions are costly only when lost.
The body has its own installment plan.

And as an extra, added feature,
you spin on the planets' carousel for free,
and with it you hitch a ride on the intergalactic blizzard,
with times so dizzying
that nothing here on Earth can even tremble.

Just take a closer look:
the table stands exactly where it stood,
the piece of paper still lies where it was spread,
through the open window comes a breath of air,
the walls reveal no terrifying cracks
through which nowhere might extinguish you.

Thoughts That Visit Me on Busy Streets

Faces.
Billions of faces on the earth's surface.
Each different, so we're told,
from those that have been and will be.
But Nature—since who really understands her?—
may grow tired of her ceaseless labors
and so repeats earlier ideas
by supplying us
with preworn faces.

Those passersby might be Archimedes in jeans,
Catherine the Great draped in resale,
some pharaoh with briefcase and glasses.

An unshod shoemaker's widow
from a still pint-sized Warsaw,
the master from the cave at Altamira
taking his grandkids to the zoo,
a shaggy Vandal en route to the museum
to gasp at past masters.

The fallen from two hundred centuries ago,
five centuries ago,
half a century ago.

One brought here in a golden carriage,
Another conveyed by extermination transport,

Montezuma, Confucius, Nebuchadnezzar,
their nannies, their laundresses, and Semiramida,
who only speaks English.

Billions of faces on the earth's surface.
My face, yours, whose —
you'll never know.
Maybe Nature has to shortchange us,
and to keep up, meet demand,
she fishes up what's been sunk
in the mirror of oblivion.

An Idea

An idea came to me
for a rhyme? a poem?
Well, fine — I say — stay awhile, we'll talk.
Tell me a little more about yourself.
So it whispered a few words in my ear.
Ah, so that's the story — I say — intriguing.
These matters have long weighed upon my heart.
But a poem about them? I don't think so.
So it whispered a few words in my ear.
It may seem that way — I reply —
but you overestimate my gifts and powers.
I wouldn't even know where to start.
So it whispered a few words in my ear.
You're wrong — I say — a short, pithy poem
is much harder than a long one.
Don't pester me, don't nag, it won't turn out.
So it whispered a few words in my ear.
All right then, I'll try, since you insist.
But don't say I didn't warn you.
I write, tear it up, and toss it out.
So it whispered a few words in my ear.
You're right — I say — there are always other poets.
Some of them can do it better.
I'll give you names and addresses.
So it whispered a few words in my ear.
Of course I'll envy them.
We envy even the weak poems.
But this one should . . . it ought to have . . .

So it whispered a few words in my ear.
Exactly, to have the qualities you've listed.
So let's change the subject.
How about a cup of coffee?

It just sighed.

And started vanishing.

And vanished.

Teenager

Me — a teenager?
If she suddenly stood, here, now, before me,
would I need to treat her as near and dear,
although she's strange to me, and distant?

Shed a tear, kiss her brow
for the simple reason
that we share a birth date?

So many dissimilarities between us
that only the bones are likely still the same,
the cranial vault, the eye sockets.

Since her eyes seem a little larger,
her eyelashes are longer, she's taller,
and the whole body is tightly sheathed
in smooth, unblemished skin.

Relatives and friends still link us, it is true,
but in her world nearly all are living,
while in mine almost no one survives
from that shared circle.

We differ so profoundly,
talk and think about completely different things.
She knows next to nothing —
but with a doggedness deserving better causes.
I know much more —
but not for sure.

She shows me poems,
written in a clear and careful script
I haven't used for years.

I read the poems, read them.
Well, maybe that one
if it were shorter
and touched up in a couple of places.
The rest do not bode well.

The conversation stumbles.
On her pathetic watch
time is still cheap and unsteady.
On mine it's far more precious and precise.

Nothing in parting, a fixed smile
and no emotion.

Only when she vanishes,
leaving her scarf in her haste.

A scarf of genuine wool,
in colored stripes
crocheted for her
by our mother.

I've still got it.

Hard Life with Memory

I'm a poor audience for my memory.
She wants me to attend her voice nonstop,
but I fidget, fuss,
listen and don't,
step out, come back, then leave again.

She wants all my time and attention.
She's got no problem when I sleep.
The day's a different matter, which upsets her.

She thrusts old letters, snapshots at me eagerly,
stirs up events both important and un-,
turns my eyes to overlooked views,
peoples them with my dead.

In her stories I'm always younger.
Which is nice, but why always the same story.
Every mirror holds different news for me.

She gets angry when I shrug my shoulders.
And takes revenge by hauling out old errors,
weighty, but easily forgotten.
Looks into my eyes, checks my reaction.
Then comforts me, it could be worse.

She wants me to live only for her and with her.
Ideally in a dark, locked room,
but my plans still feature today's sun,
clouds in progress, ongoing roads.

At times I get fed up with her.
I suggest a separation. From now to eternity.
Then she smiles at me with pity,
since she knows it would be the end of me too.

Microcosmos

When they first started looking through microscopes
a cold fear blew and it is still blowing.
Life hitherto had been frantic enough
in all its shapes and dimensions.
Which is why it created small-scale creatures,
assorted tiny worms and flies,
but at least the naked human eye
could see them.

But then suddenly beneath the glass,
foreign to a fault
and so petite,
that what they occupy in space
can only charitably be called a spot.

The glass doesn't even touch them,
they double and triple unobstructed,
with room to spare, willy-nilly.

To say they're many isn't saying much.
The stronger the microscope
the more exactly, avidly they're multiplied.

They don't even have decent innards.
They don't know gender, childhood, age.
They may not even know they are—or aren't.
Still they decide our life and death.

Some freeze in momentary stasis,
although we don't know what their moment is.
Since they're so minuscule themselves,
their duration may be
pulverized accordingly.

A wind-borne speck of dust is a meteor
from deepest space,
a fingerprint is a far-flung labyrinth,
where they may gather
for their mute parades,
their blind iliads and upanishads.

I've wanted to write about them for a long while,
but it's a tricky subject,
always put off for later
and perhaps worthy of a better poet,
even more stunned by the world than I.
But time is short. I write.

Foraminifera

Why not, let's take the Foraminifera.
They lived, since they were, and were, since they lived.
They did what they could since they were able.
In the plural since the plural,
although each one on its own,
in its own, since in its own
small limestone shell.
Time summarized them later
in layers, since layers,
without going into details,
since there's pity in the details.
And so I have before me
two views in one:
a mournful cemetery made
of tiny eternal rests
or,
rising from the sea,
the azure sea, dazzling white cliffs,
cliffs that are here because they are.

Before a Journey

They call it: space.
It's easy to define with that one word,
much harder with many.

Empty and full of everything at once?
Shut tight in spite of being open,
since nothing
can escape from it?
Inflated beyond all limits?
And if it has a limit,
what the devil does it border on?

Well, all fine and good. But go to sleep now.
It's night, tomorrow you've got more pressing matters
made to measure for you:
touching objects placed close at hand,
casting glances at the intended distance.
Listening to voices within earshot.

Then that journey from point A to point B.
Departure at 12:40 local time,
and flight above the puffs of local clouds
through whichever infinitely
fleeting strip of sky.

Divorce

For the kids the first ending of the world.
For the cat a new master.
For the dog a new mistress.
For the furniture stairs, thuds, my way or the highway.
For the walls bright squares where pictures once hung.
For the neighbors new subjects, a break in the boredom.
For the car better if there were two.
For the novels, the poems — fine, take what you want.
Worse with encyclopedias and VCRs,
not to mention the guide to proper usage,
which doubtless holds pointers on two names —
are they still linked with the conjunction "and"
or does a period divide them.

Assassins

They think for days on end,
how to kill so as to kill,
and how many killed will be many.
Apart from this they eat their meals with gusto,
pray, wash their feet, feed the birds,
make phone calls while scratching their armpits,
stanch blood when they cut a finger,
if they're women they buy sanitary napkins,
eye shadow, flowers for vases,
they make jokes on their good days,
drink citrus juice from the fridge,
watch the moon and stars at night,
place headphones with soft music on their ears
and sleep sweetly till the crack of dawn
— unless what they're thinking needs doing at night.

Example

A gale
stripped all the leaves from the trees last night
except for one leaf
left
to sway solo on a naked branch.

With this example
Violence demonstrates
that yes of course –
it likes its little joke from time to time.

Identification

It's good you came — she says.
You heard a plane crashed on Thursday?
Well, so they came to see me
about it.
The story is he was on the passenger list.
So what, he might have changed his mind.
They gave me some pills so I wouldn't fall apart.
Then they showed me I don't know who.
All black, burned except one hand.
A scrap of shirt, a watch, a wedding ring.
I got furious, that can't be him.
He wouldn't do that to me, look like that.
The stores are bursting with those shirts.
The watch is just a regular old watch.
And our names on that ring,
they're only the most ordinary names.
It's good you came. Sit here beside me.
He really was supposed to get back Thursday.
But we've got so many Thursdays left this year.
I'll put the kettle on for tea.
I'll wash my hair, then what,
try to wake up from all this.
It's good you came, since it was cold there,
and him just in some rubber sleeping bag,
him, I mean, you know, that unlucky man.
I'll put the Thursday on, wash the tea,
since our names are completely ordinary —

Nonreading

Bookstores don't provide
a remote control for Proust,
you can't switch
to a soccer match,
or a quiz show, win a Cadillac.

We live longer
but less precisely
and in shorter sentences.

We travel faster, farther, more often,
but bring back slides instead of memories.
Here I am with some guy.
There I guess that's my ex.
Here everyone's naked
so this must be a beach.

Seven volumes — mercy.
Couldn't it be cut or summarized,
or better yet put into pictures.
There was that series called "*The Doll*"
but my sister-in-law says that's some other P.*

And by the way, who was he anyway.
They say he wrote in bed for years on end.
Page after page
at a snail's pace.
But we're still going in fifth gear
and, knock on wood, never better.

* The reference is to the Polish novelist Bolesław Prus (1847–1912), whose most famous work, *The Doll* (1890), later became a popular TV miniseries. (*Translators' note*)

Portrait from Memory

Everything seems to agree.
The head's shape, the features, the silhouette, the height.
But there's no resemblance.
Maybe not in that position?
A different color scheme?
Maybe more in profile,
as if looking at something?
What about something in his hands?
His own book? Someone else's?
A map? Binoculars? A fishing reel?
And should he be wearing something different?
A soldier's uniform in '39? Camp stripes?
A windbreaker from that closet?
Or — as if passing to the other shore —
up to his ankles, his knees, his waist, his neck,
deluged? Naked?
And maybe a backdrop should be added?
For example, a meadow still uncut?
Rushes? Birches? A lovely cloudy sky?
Maybe someone should be next to him?
Arguing with him? Joking?
Drinking? Playing cards?
A relative? A chum?
Several women? One?
Maybe standing in a window?
Going out the door?
With a stray dog at his feet?
In a friendly crowd?
No, no, all wrong.

He should be alone,
that suits some best.
And not so familiar, so close up?
Farther? Even farther?
In the furthermost depths of the image?
His voice couldn't carry
even if he called?
And what in the foreground?
Oh, anything.
As long as it's a bird
just flying by.

Dreams

Despite the geologists' knowledge and craft,
mocking magnets, graphs and maps —
in a split second the dream
piles before us mountains as stony
as real life.

And if mountains, then valleys, plains
with perfect infrastructures.
Without engineers, contractors, workers,
bulldozers, diggers, or supplies —
raging highways, instant bridges,
thickly populated pop-up cities.

Without directors, megaphones, and cameramen —
crowds knowing exactly when to frighten us
and when to vanish.

Without architects deft in their craft,
without carpenters, bricklayers, concrete pourers —
on the path a sudden house just like a toy,
and in it vast halls that echo with our steps
and walls constructed out of solid air.

Not only the scale, it's also the precision —
a specific watch, an entire fly,
on the table a cloth with cross-stitched flowers,
a bitten apple with teeth marks.

And we — unlike circus acrobats,
conjurers, wizards, and hypnotists —
can fly unfledged,
we light dark tunnels with our eyes,
we wax eloquent in unknown tongues,
talking not with just anyone, but with the dead.

And as a bonus, despite our own freedom,
the choices of our heart, our tastes,
we're swept away
by amorous yearnings for —
and the alarm clock rings.

So what can they tell us, the writers of dreambooks,
the scholars of oneiric signs and omens,
the doctors with couches for analyses —
if anything fits,
it's accidental,
and for one reason only,
that in our dreamings,
in their shadowings and gleamings,
in their multiplings, inconceivablings,
in their haphazardings and widescatterings
at times even a clear-cut meaning
may slip through.

In a Mail Coach

My imagination sentenced me to this journey.
Boxes and packages get drenched on the mail coach roof.
Inside crush, hubbub, stuffiness.
There's a stout sweaty hausfrau,
a hunter swathed in pipe smoke with a dead hare,
l'abbé snores, a demijohn of wine clasped in his arms,
a nursemaid holds an infant red from bawling,
a tipsy merchant with relentless hiccups,
a lady irritated for all the reasons above,
furthermore a boy with a trumpet,
a large fleabitten dog,
and a caged parrot.

And also the person I got on for,
almost invisible amid the others' bundles,
but he's there, and he's called Juliusz Słowacki.*

He's clearly none too eager for a chat.
He draws a letter from a crumpled envelope,
it's doubtless been read many times before,
since the pages fray along the edges.
When a dried violet drops from the sheets
ah! we both sigh and seize it in flight.

Perhaps it's a good time to tell him
what I've planned long ago in my thoughts.
Excuse me, sir, but it's urgent and important.

* One of Poland's greatest Romantic poets, Słowacki lived from 1809 to 1849. (*Translators' note*)

I've come from the Future and I know how it turns out.
Your poems are loved and admired
and you lie with kings in Wawel Castle.

Alas my imagination lacks the power
to make him hear or at least see me.
He doesn't even feel me tug his sleeve.
He calmly slips the violet between the sheets,
which go back into the envelope, and then into a trunk,
glances through the rain-streaked window,
rises, pins his cloak, squeezes to the door,
and what else? Gets off at the next station.

I keep him in my sight a few more minutes.
He walks off, so slight with that trunk of his,
plows on, head down,
like one who knows
no one is waiting.

Now only the extras remain.
An extended clan beneath umbrellas,
a corporal with a whistle, breathless recruits in tow,
a wagon full of piglets,
and two fresh horses waiting to be hitched.

Ella in Heaven

She prayed to God
with all her heart
to make her
a happy white girl.
And if it's too late for such changes,
then at least, Lord God, see what I weigh,
subtract at least half of me.
But the good God answered No.
He just put his hand on her heart,
checked her throat, stroked her head.
But when everything is over — He added —
you'll give me joy by coming to me,
my black comfort, my well-sung stump.

Vermeer

So long as that woman from the Rijksmuseum
in painted quiet and concentration
keeps pouring milk day after day
from the pitcher to the bowl
the World hasn't earned
the world's end.

Metaphysics

It's been and gone.
It's been, so it's gone.
In the same irreversible order,
for such is the rule of this foregone game.
A trite conclusion, not worth writing
if it weren't an unquestionable fact,
a fact for ever and ever,
for the whole cosmos, as it is and will be,
that something really was
until it was gone,
even the fact
that today you had a side of fries.

ENOUGH

2011

Someone I've Been Watching for a While

He doesn't arrive en masse.
Doesn't gather gregariously.
Doesn't convene communally.
Doesn't celebrate congenially.

Doesn't wrest from himself
a choral voice.
Doesn't declare to all concerned.
Doesn't affirm in the name.
Investigations aren't conducted
in his presence —
who's for, and who's against,
thank you, none opposed.

His head is missing
where head meets head,
step in step, shoulder to shoulder
and ever onward nonstop
with a pocketful of leaflets
and a product made of hops.

Where it's sweetness and light
only to start,
since one crowd quickly
mixes with the next,
and who is to say
on the following day,
whose flowers, whose bricks,
whose huzzahs, whose sticks.

Unremarked.
Unspectacular.
He's employed by City Sanitation.
At first light
from the site of the event
he sweeps up, carries off, tosses in the truck,
what's been hammered onto half-dead trees,
trampled into the exhausted grass.

Tattered banners,
broken bottles,
burned effigies,
gnawed bones,
rosaries, whistles, and condoms.

Once he found a dove cage in the bushes.
He took it home
so he could
keep it empty.

Confessions of a Reading Machine

I, Number Three Plus Four Divided by Seven,
am renowned for my vast linguistic knowledge.
I now recognize thousands of languages
employed by extinct people
in their histories.

Everything that they recorded with their signs,
even when crushed under layers of disasters,
I extract, reconstruct
in its original form.

Not to boast,
but I even read lava
and scan ashes.

I explain on a screen
each object mentioned,
when it was produced,
and what from, and what for.

And solely on my own initiative,
I peruse the occasional letter
and correct its
spelling errors.

I admit — certain words
do cause me difficulty.
For example I still cannot explain precisely
the states called "feelings."

Likewise "soul," a peculiar expression.
I've determined for now that it is a kind of fog
purportedly more lasting than mortal organisms.

But the word "am" gives me the most trouble.
It appears to be an ordinary function,
conducted daily, but not collectively,
in the present prehistoric tense,
specifically, in the continuous,
although as we know discontinued long ago.

But will this do for a definition?
I feel rumbling in my linkages and grinding of my screws.
My button to Head Office smokes but won't light up.

Perhaps my pal Two Fifths of Zero Fractured by Half
will provide brotherly assistance.
True, he's a known lunatic,
but he's got ideas.

There Are Those Who

There are those who conduct life more precisely.
They keep order within and around them.
A way for everything, and a right answer.

They guess straight off who's with who, who's got who,
to what end, in what direction.

They set their stamp on single truths,
toss unnecessary facts into the shredder
and unfamiliar persons
into previously designated files.

They think as long as it takes,
not a second more,
since doubt lies lurking behind that second.

And when they're dismissed from existence,
they leave their place of work
through the appropriately marked exit.

Sometimes I envy them
— it passes, luckily.

Chains

A scorching day, a doghouse and a dog on a chain.
A full dish of water a few steps off.
But the chain is too short and the dog can't reach.
Let's add one more detail to the picture,
the much longer,
less visible chains
that allow us freely to pass by.

At the Airport

They run to each other with open arms,
laughing, calling: At last! At last!
Both in heavy winter wraps,
thick caps,
scarves,
gloves,
boots,
but only for us.
For each other — naked.

Compulsion

We eat another life so as to live.
A corpse of pork with departed cabbage.
Every menu is an obituary.

Even the kindest of souls
must consume, digest something killed
so that their warm hearts
won't stop beating.

Even the most lyrical of poets.
Even the strictest ascetics
chew and swallow something
that once kept itself growing.

I can't quite reconcile this with good gods.
Unless they're naïve,
unless they're gullible,
and gave all power over the world to nature.
And she, frenzied, sends us hunger,
and where hunger begins,
innocence ends.

Hunger instantly joins forces with the senses:
taste, smell, and touch, and sight,
since we don't fail to notice what dishes
are served on which plates.

Even hearing plays a part
in what takes place,
since cheerful chatter often rises at the table.

Everyone Sometime

Everyone sometime has somebody close die,
between to be or not to be
he's forced to choose the latter.

We can't admit that it's a mundane fact,
subsumed in the course of events,
in accordance with procedure:

sooner or later on the daily docket,
the evening, late night, or first dawn docket;

and explicit as an entry in an index,
as a statute in a codex,
as any chance date
on a calendar.

But such is the right and left of nature.
Such, willy-nilly, is her omen and her amen.
Such are her instruments and omnipotence.

And only on occasion
a small favor on her part—
she tosses our dead loved ones
into dreams.

Hand

Twenty-seven bones,
thirty-five muscles,
around two thousand nerve cells
in every tip of all five fingers.
It’s more than enough
to write *Mein Kampf*
or *Pooh Corner.*

Mirror

Yes, I remember that wall
in our demolished town.
It jutted almost up to the fifth floor.
A mirror hung on the fourth,
an impossible mirror,
unshattered, firmly attached.

It didn't reflect anybody's face,
no hands arranging hair,
no door across the room,
nothing you could call
a place.

As if it were on vacation —
the living sky gazed in it,
busy clouds in the wild air,
the dust of rubble washed by shining rains,
birds in flight, stars, sunrises.

And like any well-made object,
it functioned flawlessly,
with an expert lack of astonishment.

While Sleeping

I dreamed I was looking for something,
maybe hidden somewhere or lost
under the bed, under the stairs,
under an old address.

I dug through wardrobes, boxes and drawers
pointlessly packed with stuff and nonsense.

I pulled from my suitcases
the years and journeys I'd picked up.

I shook from my pockets
withered letters, litter, leaves not addressed to me.

I ran panting
through comforting, discomfiting
displaces, places.

I floundered through tunnels of snow
and unremembrance.

I got stuck in thorny thickets
and conjectures.

I swam through air
and the grass of childhood.

I hustled to finish up
before the outdated dusk fell,
the curtain, silence.

In the end I stopped knowing
what I'd been looking for so long.

I woke up.
Looked at my watch.
The dream took not quite two and a half minutes.

Such are the tricks to which time resorts
ever since it started stumbling
on sleeping heads.

Reciprocity

There are catalogs of catalogs.
There are poems about poems.
There are plays about actors played by actors.
Letters due to letters.
Words used to clarify words.
Brains occupied with studying brains.
There are griefs as infectious as laughter.
Papers emerging from waste papers.
Seen glances.
Conditions conditioned by the conditional.
Large rivers with major contributions from small ones.
Forests grown over and above by forests.
Machines designed to make machines.
Dreams that wake us suddenly from dreams.
Health needed for regaining health.
Stairs leading as much up as down.
Glasses for finding glasses.
Inspiration born of expiration.
And even if only from time to time
hatred of hatred.
All in all,
ignorance of ignorance
and hands employed to wash hands.

To My Own Poem

Best case scenario —
you'll be, my poem, read attentively,
discussed, remembered.

Worst comes to worst,
only read.

A third option —
actually written,
but tossed into the trash a moment later.

The fourth and final possibility —
you slip away unwritten,
happily humming something to yourself.

Map

Flat as the table
it's placed on.
Nothing moves beneath it
and it seeks no outlet.
Above — my human breath
creates no stirring air
and leaves its total surface
undisturbed.

Its plains, valleys are always green,
uplands, mountains are yellow and brown,
while seas, oceans remain a kindly blue
beside the tattered shores.

Everything here is small, near, accessible.
I can press volcanoes with my fingertip,
stroke the poles without thick mittens,
I can with a single glance
encompass every desert
with the river lying just beside it.

A few trees stand for ancient forests,
you couldn't lose your way among them.

In the east and west,
above and below the equator —
quiet like pins dropping,
and in every black pinprick
people keep on living.
Mass graves and sudden ruins
are out of the picture.

Nations' borders are barely visible
as if they wavered — to be or not.

I like maps, because they lie.
Because they give no access to the vicious truth.
Because great-heartedly, good-naturedly
they spread before me a world
not of this world.

Translator's Afterword

Szymborska addresses a late verse to a poem that may itself be "tossed into the trash a moment later." Most of her poems ended their careers in just this way, according to longtime friends: they never made it as far as the printed page. Szymborska herself never compiled her own Collected Poems. But the various Polish Selected Poems over the years suggest what such a volume might have looked like. She continued to winnow the work even after it had appeared in one collection or another. The purely comic works—the limericks, the "nursery rhymes" (*rymowanki*), the "eavesdroppings" (*posłuchańce*), and so on—were kept strictly segregated from the poems proper. We've followed her lead in this.

She also excluded most of her early poetry. Here too we've followed her lead. Marina Tsvetaeva speaks of "poets with a history and poets without a history." Szymborska was a poet with a history in Tsvetaeva's sense. It took her three volumes—an unpublished postwar collection and two Socialist Realist volumes from the early fifties—to become the poet Wisława Szymborska, or so her own editing suggests. We have translated all the early poems that she continued to include in one Selected Poems after another. And we have translated virtually all the poems from her published collections beginning with *Calling Out to Yeti* (1957), with the exception of a very few poems that Szymborska herself conceded were untranslatable. "You're lucky," she said about one of them, "you only wasted three weeks on it. It took the Dutch translator six months to give up."

I began this project many years ago with my beloved friend, teacher, and mentor, the magnificent poet Stanisław Barańczak. I've had to finish it without him. In recent years his health has not permitted him to continue the collaboration that has been one of the great joys of my life. As I worked on alone, I asked myself continuously, "Would it be good enough for Stanisław?" I hope so.

You don't work so long on a poet without accruing a great many—generally wonderful—debts. Our extraordinary editor, Drenka Willen, took a chance on a little-known poet with an unpronounceable name several years before the Nobel Prize made Szymborska famous. She did it because she loved the poems, which Charles Simic first gave her in our English incarnation. Drenka's critical acuity and her boundless sympathy for translators have buoyed us through the decades. How would I have made it through this volume without Drenka's intelligence, her patience, her perfect pitch? I'll never know. Several friends whom I met when I first met Szymborska herself, in Stockholm in 1996, have been invaluable guides through the years. Michał Rusinek, Tadeusz Nyczek, Krystyna and Ryszard Krynicki—all have aided, abetted, and assisted me in more ways than I can name. I'm indebted, too, to Larry Cooper's meticulous editing in the final stages of this project.

I could name many others. But I'll conclude with just a few. The first is my best friend, our most ruthless critic, and our biggest fan, the dear and splendid Ania Barańczak. Then there are Mike and Martin Lopez. My son Martin was two when I met Wisława, and for many years I gave them the same presents. He outgrew them. She never did.

An old friend once inscribed his scholarly book on Szymborska's poetry as follows: "To Wisława, without whom this book could not have been written." Here is my variation on his theme: "To Wisława, without whom this book would not exist. Thank you."

—*Clare Cavanagh*

Translation Credits

Poems translated by Clare Cavanagh

Once we had the world backwards and forwards . . . ; Leaving the Movie Theater; Comic Love Poem; Black Song; In Trite Rhymes; Circus Animals; Questions You Ask Yourself; Lovers; Key; Night; Hania; Flagrance; Moment of Silence; Rehabilitation; I hear trumpets play the tune . . . ; Midsummer Night's Dream; Dream; Poem in Honor; A Note; Pursuit; Nothingness unseamed itself for me too . . . ; The Old Turtle's Dream; Military Parade; Apple Tree; Consolation; The Old Professor; Perspective; The Poet's Nightmare; Distraction; Someone I've Been Watching for a While; Confessions of a Reading Machine; There Are Those Who; Chains; At the Airport; Compulsion; Everyone Sometime; Hand; Mirror; While Sleeping; Reciprocity; To My Own Poem; Map

Poems translated by Clare Cavanagh and Stanisław Barańczak

Nothing Twice; Buffo; Commemoration; Classifieds; To My Friends; Funeral (I); Brueghel's Two Monkeys; Still; Greeting the Supersonics; Still Life with a Balloon; Notes from a Nonexistent Himalayan Expedition; An Effort; Four A.M.; Atlantis; I'm Working on the World; The Monkey; Lesson; Museum; A Moment in Troy; Shadow; The Rest; Clochard; Vocabulary; Travel Elegy; Without a Title; An Unexpected Meeting; Golden Anniversary; Starvation Camp Near Jaslo; Parable; Ballad; Over Wine; Rubens' Women; Coloratura; Bodybuilders' Contest; Poetry Reading; Epitaph; Prologue to a Comedy; Likeness; I am too close . . . ; The Tower of Babel; Water; Synopsis; In Heraclitus's River; Conversation with a Stone; The Joy of Writing; Memory Finally; Landscape; Family Album; Laughter; The Railroad Station; Alive; Born; Census; Soliloquy for Cassandra; A Byzantine Mosaic; Beheading; Pietà; Innocence; Vietnam; Written in a Hotel; A Film from the Sixties; Report from the Hospital; Returning Birds; Thomas Mann; Tarsier; To My Heart, on Sunday; The Acrobat; A Paleolithic Fertility Fetish; Cave; Motion; No End of Fun; Could Have; Falling from the Sky; Wrong Number; Theater Impressions; Voices; The Letters of the Dead; Old Folks' Home; Advertisement; Lazarus Takes a Walk; Snapshot of a Crowd; Going Home; Discovery; Dinosaur Skeleton; A Speech at the Lost-and-Found; Astonishment; Birthday; Interview with a Child; Allegro ma Non Troppo; Autotomy; Frozen Motion; Certainty; The Classic; In Praise of Dreams; True Love; Under One Small Star; A Large Number; Thank-You Note; Psalm; Lot's Wife; Seen from Above; Experiment; Smiles; The Terrorist, He's Watching; A Medieval Miniature; Aging Opera Singer; In Praise of My Sister; Hermitage; Portrait of a Woman; Evaluation of an Unwritten Poem; Warning; The Onion; The Suicide's Room; In Praise of Feeling Bad about Yourself; Life While-You-Wait; On the Banks of the Styx; Utopia; Pi; Stage Fright; Surplus; Archeology; View with a Grain of Sand; Clothes; On Death, Without Exaggeration; The Great Man's House; In Broad Daylight; Our Ancestors' Short Lives; Hitler's First Photograph; The Century's Decline; Children of Our Age; Tortures; Plotting with the Dead; Writing a Résumé; Funeral (II); An Opinion on the Question of Pornography; A Tale Begun; Into the Ark; Possibilities; Miracle Fair; The People on the Bridge; Sky; No Title Required; Some People Like Poetry; The End and the Beginning; Hatred; Reality Demands; The Real World; Elegiac Calculation; Cat in an Empty Apartment; Parting with a View; Séance; Love at First Sight; May 16, 1973; Maybe All This; Slapstick; Nothing's a Gift; One Version of Events; We're Extremely Fortunate; Moment; Among the Multitudes; Clouds; Negative; Receiver; The Three Oddest Words; The Silence of Plants; Plato, or Why; A Little Girl Tugs at the Tablecloth; A Memory; Puddle; First Love; A Few Words on the Soul; Early Hour; In the Park; A Contribution to Statistics; Some People; Photograph from September 11; Return Baggage; The Ball; A Note; List; Everything; Absence; ABC; Highway Accident; The Day After — Without Us; An Occurrence; The Courtesy of the Blind; Monologue of a Dog Ensnared in History; An Interview with Atropos; Labyrinth; Greek Statue; In Fact Every Poem; Here; Thoughts That Visit Me on Busy Streets; An Idea; Teenager; Hard Life with Memory; Microcosmos; Foraminifera; Before a Journey; Divorce; Assassins; Example; Identification; Nonreading; Portrait from Memory; Dreams; In a Mail Coach; Ella in Heaven; Vermeer; Metaphysics

Index of Titles and First Lines

CPSIA information can be obtained
at www.ICGtesting.com
Printed in the USA
LVHW041557200521
688017LV00009B/1626

9 780544 705159